Mother of Detective Fiction

Mother of Detective Fiction:

The Life and Works
of
Anna Katharine Green

Patricia D. Maida

Bowling Green State University Popular Press
Bowling Green, Ohio 43403

For Peter and Damon

Photo of Anna Katharine Green
Courtesy of Mary Alice Rohlfs

Acknowledgements

I am endebted to Mary Alice Rohlfs (Mrs. Roland Rohlfs) who has kept the memory of Anna Katharine Green alive. Her generosity with materials and data from her mother-in-law's estate provided the foundation for this project. It is her vivid memory and gentle wit that inform these pages.

I am also grateful to my mother, Theresa Dinneen, for assistance with the New York material; to my colleagues at the University of the District of Columbia for listening and advising; and to my husband, Peter Maida, for his expert tutelage in word processing.

Contents

Foreword   1
Chapter One
    The Leavenworth Case (1878)   4
Chapter Two
    The Shaping of a Writer   18
Chapter Three
    Choices   31
Chapter Four
    Conventions and Influence   46
Chapter Five
    Detectives   56
Chapter Six
    Sin and Crime   78
Chapter Seven
    Women's Rights and Roles   89
Afterword   104
Notes   106
Bibliography   114
Index   117

Foreword

    After cornering the American market with best-selling novels of detection, Anna Katharine Green earned the title "Mother of Detective Fiction." Although other writers had written mystery fiction before her, Green was recognized as the female stylist who helped to shape detective fiction into the classic form we see today. As Alma Murch observes in *The Development of the Detective Novel,* ... in "Green's work we can discern for the first time, in its entirety, the pattern that became characteristic of most English detective novels written during the following fifty years" (159). During her long and prolific career, Green produced thirty-five novels as well as short fiction, poetry, and drama.

    With the publication of *The Leavenworth Case* in 1878, Green attained international recognition. She then proceeded to refine elements of the genre: the puzzle, the environment, and the detective. Her special contribution, however, was the development of a series detective—Ebenezer Gryce of the New York Metropolitan Police Force who appeared almost a decade before Arthur Conan Doyle's Sherlock Holmes. Gryce captured the imagination of thousands who clamored for additional adventures featuring the unassuming Mr. Gryce. Like Agatha Christie's Poirot, Gryce became so popular that his creator found herself rejuvenating him in order to fulfill reader demands. Along with Gryce, Green introduced Amelia Butterworth and Violet Strange, two female series sleuths. Butterworth became the prototype for the clever but nosey spinster, whose descendants include Agatha Christie's Jane Marple, Mary Roberts Rinehart's Rachel Innis, and Patricia Wentworth's Maud

Silver. Violet Strange, a young private detective, inspired the beginnings of the "girl" detective.

To nineteenth century readers, Green offered a challenging puzzle and well developed characters. Men, as well as women, delighted in her imaginative conundrums as they joined in the game of detection. (She did not wish to be considered a woman's writer.) While observing the conventions of detective fiction, Green moved beyond the constraints of form to develop both environment and character. She painted city and rural family life—frequently offering glimpses of New York's Fifth Avenue society. Just as writers Wilkie Collins and Emile Gaboriau had glamorized the aristocracy of England and France, Green portrayed America's elite and their new wealth. She focused on social issues, on the differences in the lifestyles of the well-to-do and the lower class; and on moral issues, presenting Hawthornesque tales of good and evil.

Green forged the links in the American school of detective fiction between Edgar Allan Poe and contemporary authors, enriching the tradition and providing mystery as well as insight for readers past and present. Modern readers may still read Green's work for plot and characterization, but as social history her fiction is even more significant. The environment of New York at the turn of the century, the roles men and women played, and the socio-political dynamics of family and community are dramatically portrayed in Green's stories.

In examining the work of a prolific writer, one chooses a focus and of necessity must select from the range of works appropriate texts for closer study. Thus with Anna Katharine Green, this study will begin with her first novel, *The Leavenworth Case*. At the time of its publication in 1878, Green was unknown. As we look back upon the factors which shaped her life and writing, a distinct personality emerges—an educated, well-disciplined woman. Her life was not privileged. She had to work hard, experiencing disappointment along with personal satisfaction. Nevertheless, she perceived herself as a professional writer at a time when women were often forced into writing as an avocation. The choices she made as a professional writer are as significant as her contribution to the development of detective fiction. And her perspective on the emerging values and social constructs of American society offers insights to the modern reader.

Chapter One
The Leavenworth Case

In 1878, a young woman took the Fifth Avenue Coach to George Putnam's publishing house on lower Broadway. She was carrying a heavy parcel wrapped in a shawl strap—a 145,000 word manuscript. The woman was Anna Katharine Green, a thirty-two year old New Yorker. The manuscript was *The Leavenworth Case*, the first detective novel written by an American woman to be published in a single volume (Murch 158). It was to become a seminal work, winning for its author the title—Mother of Detective Fiction.

Though Miss Green was totally unknown at the time, response to the novel was overwhelming: it eventually sold over a million copies.[1] Twenty-five years later, "its publishers announced that they had worn out two sets of plates reprinting the regular edition and were making another set" (Mott 63). Among the more celebrated writers to praise Green was Wilkie Collins whose approval helped to publicize the book: "Her powers of invention are so remarkable— she has so much imagination and so much belief (a most important qualification for our art) in what she says.... Dozens of times in reading the story I have stopped to admire the fertility of invention, the delicate treatment of incident—and the fine perception of event on the personages of the story..." (152). Although Green's imaginative powers were essential to her success, other practical factors may have contributed more—the increasing popular appeal of detective fiction and the glamor of the New York environment. She chose a field that was burgeoning with opportunity, and she was fortunate in contracting with George Putnam. By giving the

novel an aristocratic New York setting, she also captured the interest
of those eager to read about the closed world of high society.

Detective fiction was becoming a popular genre, but there were
other literary forms which might have provided a start for a novice
writer. Green might have followed the path of literati like Cooper,
Irving, Scott, or Dumas. Or she might have joined forces with those
writing for the women's market. Novels written by and for women
which appealed "to the senses—to pity, fear, and horror," were
flooding the market here and abroad, numbering among them *East
Lynne* (1861) by Mrs. Henry Wood and *Lady Audley's Secret* (1862)
by Mary Elizabeth Braddon (Mann 26). Magazines such as *The
Ladies Companion* and *The Ladies World* offered serial novels to
masses of female subscribers. Another option might have been the
dime novel—a paper edition catering to the tastes and pocketbooks
of the general public. These low-priced editions had cornered the
market with wild west narratives in the 1860s, but mystery fiction
was gradually becoming the vogue (Bragin 1). The celebrated "Old
Sleuth" stories which featured a serial amateur detective captured
the attention of dime novel enthusiasts. Under the pseudonym of
Old Sleuth, Harlan P. Halsey was publishing stories in a periodical
entitled *The Fireside Companion* as early as 1872, before beginning
the Old Sleuth Library of dime novels (Pearson 192). But Green
did not choose any of these markets. Though her writing contains
features similar to the women's literature of the day, Murch points
out the difference: "In some respects Miss Green's novels resemble
those of Mrs. Henry Wood and Miss Braddon in their introduction
of such melodramatic features as guilty secrets behind a facade of
wealth and luxury, unjust suspicions, dramatic revelations and
noble reconciliations, but Miss Green uses them merely to provide
background and create the mystery" (Murch 158). Eschewing the
dime novel, modeling her work on the quality detective fiction
available in the 1860s and 1870s, Green wrote for the mass market.

Miss Green was taking a risk, entering a field that was considered
male territory. As Murch points out, "Mid-nineteenth century
publishers seemed to feel there was something peculiarly indelicate

about tales of crime or criminals being written by a woman, and were reluctant to print them, though stories of social or domestic life were readily accepted" (152). However, George Putnam was among the few publishers who developed positive business relationships with female authors, especially those, like Green, who espoused values of "Victorian morality" (Coultrap-McQuin 8). Fortunately, when Green published her first detective story, the American market was ready, in fact, waiting for such a story: New York millionaire found murdered in the library of his Fifth Avenue home. *The Leavenworth Case* opened up the culture of Manhattan's elite society to public scrutiny. Readers clamored for a look inside the Leavenworth's opulent home, and they participated in the chase for the murderer.

Green's novel was significant. Although the detective novel was flourishing in Europe, America had produced no significant heirs to Edgar Allan Poe whose short stories marked the beginning of the genre in the 1840s. In his history of detective fiction, Haycraft contends that "American fields lay fallow from Poe's "Purloined Letter" (1844) to Anna Katharine Green's *The Leavenworth Case* (1878)" (83). But Green did not adopt Poe's short story form or his detective, M. Auguste Dupin—an upper class, intellectual Frenchman. Instead she made an original contribution, choosing the novel as her form, America as her setting, and an American policeman as her detective.

Green knew Poe's work and used conventions that he developed, but admittedly her model was the French novelist, Emile Gaboriau (Woodward 168). *L'Affaire Lerouge*, Gaboriau's first detective novel, appeared in 1863 in French, then in translation, and later in pirated editions in the United States (Bleiber xx). From his experience as a court reporter, Gaboriau transformed fact into fiction and made detection a credible art. He was able to weave family scandal, identity shifts, and murder with technical data so that the scientific analysis of crime became his trademark. Green gave *The Leavenworth Case* the sub-title—"A Lawyer's Story"; this caption is similar to the term Gaboriau applied to his work—"le roman judiciare." The sub-title for Green, however, was more than a link to Gaboriau. She was not only emulating him, but also distinguishing her work from the "ladies' novels" of the day. The "lawyer's story" is told from the point of view of a young attorney, guided by a professional law enforcement officer. Like Gaboriau who was interested in forensic science, Green uses ballistics, scientific analysis of clues, and medical reports in her novel—a touch which was unexpected of female writers of her day.

From Gaboriau, Green may also have drawn some of the characteristics of her serial detective, Inspector Ebenezer Gryce, who makes his first appearance in *The Leavenworth Case*. In his capacity as a member of the police establishment, he bears some kinship to M. Lecoq—Gaboriau's police hero. In personality, though, he is more like Gaboriau's Pere Tabaret—grandfatherly, unassuming, and insightful. Yet there is nothing Gallic about Ebenezer Gryce—he is clearly an American. As the narrator of *The Leavenworth Case* emphasizes, "Mr. Gryce, the detective, was not the thin, wirey individual with a shrewd eye that seems to plunge into the core of your being and pounce at once upon its hidden secret.... Mr. Gryce was a portly, comfortable personage with an eye that never pounced, that did not even rest—on you. If it rested anywhere, it was always on some insignificant object in your vicinity..." (7). By giving Gryce a reticent facade, with his odd way of looking at people, Green was disassociating him from his predecessors. The humanistic treatment of Inspector Gryce follows the tradition of Charles Dickens' Inspector Bucket and Wilkie Collins' Sargeant Cuff. Both Dickens and Collins offer sympathetic treatments of police figures, reflecting respect for the policeman and his role in society. Green may have been directly influenced by Dickens and Collins, but their influence was reinforced by her impressions of policemen whom she was able to observe first hand in New York City.[2]

The timeliness of detective fiction as a viable literary form contributed to Green's success. If the beginning of the nineteenth century was characterized by the flowering of poetry, the end of the century was dominated by fiction. Within the broad perspective of the novel, detective fiction bridged the gap between the romantic and the realistic. Society was looking for stability and control in a changing society. Industrialization had transformed communities and produced new values. Changing social standards spawned a nationalistic effort, particularly among the middle class, to avert the erosion of native ideals. Crime, according to Davis, was viewed by many American writers as a "betrayal of a pure and noble heritage" (Davis 251). The detective became the problem-solver—like the medieval knight who dedicated his life to restoring order. Readers were more than willing to fantasize about the powers of a detective who could put their world back together, especially one who was admitted to the closed and protected world of the upper class.

With its glamour, its fascinating upper class, its contrasts and energies, New York City was a likely choice for the setting of Anna Katharine Green's first detective story. Readers who followed New York's high society, its debutantes and lavish dress balls, were eager to catch a glimpse of life behind the doors of Fifth Avenue's brownstones. In his classic history of New York, James D. McCabe observed, "Extravagance is the besetting sin of New York society. Money is absolutely thrown away. Fortunes are spent every year in dress and in all sorts of follies. Houses are fitted up and furnished in the most sumptuous style, the building and its contents being sometimes worth a million dollars" (Longstreet 66). It was just the right kind of society for crime, and it was the right place for a mystery novel. The Leavenworth house has the attributes that would captivate readers; the narrator describes "the gorgeous house, its elaborate furnishing, the little glimpses of yesterday's life as seen in the open piano with its sheet of music held in place by a lady's dainty fan...the glow of satin, glitter of bronze and glimmer of marble...." (12). Thus Green offered masses of middle class readers the opportunity to enter this closed society and to play the "game" of solving the mystery puzzle.

In order to appreciate Green's point of view, it is important to understand her position as a member of the middle class. Consider the contrast between Green and another literary figure whose family was included in New York's social register—Edith Jones Wharton.[3] In 1879, the year after the publication of *The Leavenworth Case*, Edith Jones made her debut at the private home of a well known millionaire on Fifth Avenue near Forty-second Street. Her family had the background and the home typical of the upper class: "the Jones' narrow-fronted, three story brownstone was on West 23rd Street near Fifth Avenue. Passing up the inevitable Dutch stoop, one encountered a vestibule painted in Pompein red, and beyond it the first of several cramped sitting rooms. The white and gold drawing room on the second floor was rigorously protected from the world outside by two layers of curtains: sashes, lace draperies, and damask hangings. Heavy pieces of Dutch marquetry adorned it, and a cabinet displayed a number of old painted fans and exquisite and never-used pieces of old lace brought back from Venice and Paris" (Lewis 22). Miss Green was not a debutante, nor did her family own a luxurious home. While young Edith Jones was tutored at home, Anna attended public schools before graduating from a private college for women. Edith Jones spent her summers in Newport and her winters in Europe; Anna summered with her cousins in East Haddam, Connecticut and went to Europe only once, in 1890. The experiences of these two women were totally different, as was their literary expression. Where Wharton described the psycho-social plight of the upper class as an insider, Green focused on the luxury, the economic and moral vulnerability of the same society as an outsider.

Though Green was an outsider, she was an astute observer. She was living in Manhattan when she wrote her first novel and was well acquainted with the city and its populace. After graduating from Ripley College in Vermont in 1866, Anna rejoined her family in rented quarters at 34 Murray Street in the Murray Hill section of Manhattan. Through her attorney father's connections with law-makers in the city, she had a pipeline to the details of local crime.

Information that she did not get at home was available in newspapers which featured society as well as sensational crime news: "Readers of newspapers could turn from an account of some sumptuous banquet at Delmonico's restaurant in New York, or some gilded ball in Newport, to a record of the police charging half-starved working-men, or a description of want and disease in the congested tenements" (Nevins 201). Detective fiction effectively combined the kind of news that had the greatest appeal—society column gossip and front page crime. As Green was to explain in an article written for *The American Magazine*, she calculated that detective fiction would appeal to newspaper readers (39).

The press encouraged readers to follow the adventures of New York's most elite group, "the 400"—a clique composed of well-established socialites. "The good old families," according to George Curtis of *Harper's Weekly*, possessed "virtue and age...the chief qualities of perhaps the only aristocracy New York would ever know" (Lewis 22). It was in the 1870s that Mrs. Astor engaged Ward McAllister as her social secretary, and it was McAllister who was to choose the "Patriarchs," the twenty-five young men of old money and good breeding who would "create and lead society" (Horton 2-3). A total of 400 persons emerged from the nucleus of the Patriarchs to be numbered among New York's aristocracy. 400 was reputed to be the magic number because what was the maximum number of persons who could fit into Mrs. Astor's ballroom. The nouveaux riches were excluded; it was not until 1883 that Mrs. Astor conceded to have the rich but "new" Mrs. Vanderbilt as her guest. The 400 set the pace for all social climbers; and for those who would never attain such status, the 400 fulfilled their fantasies. Ordinary people waited to read the daily newspapers to keep up with their adventures. Consequently, although today's readers might consider Green's rendering of nineteenth century life highly romantic, if anything, it was realistic. The snobbery, elitism, and fear of scandal basic to their self-imposed social code made the upper class prime subjects for detective fiction.

But Green also captured the variety of people—the lower, the middle, and upper class, who were part of the growing metropolis. Nevins indicates that "as the cities grew and immigrants poured in (more than 5,000,000 in the decade 1880-90), they naturally became a melting pot of different races. By 1890 New York...had twice as many Irish as Dublin, two and a half times as many Jews as Warsaw, as many Germans as Hamburg, and half as many Italians as Naples" (Nevins 200). In the Leavenworth household, for example, the immigrant servants are portrayed in appropriate roles, speaking with accents and displaying the manners of their culture. All the servants are Irish immigrants: Thomas Dougherty, the butler; Katherine Malone, the cook; Molly O'Flanagan, the up-stairs girl; and Hannah Chester, the ladies' maid. In contrast, Mr. Leavenworth's private secretary, James Trueman Harwell, is a middle class American, displaying his status with "...a certain self-possession in his carriage" (27). The lines of class are clearly distinguished, as was the case in the typical wealthy home.

While the environment of the wealthy Leavenworth home enticed many a reader, the puzzle at the heart of the story provided the necessary challenge for avid readers of mystery fiction. The novel follows the traditional pattern of a detective story: that is, a crime occurs and an investigation unfolds under the supervision of a detective. Murch indicates that Green's execution of the pattern for detective fiction set the standard for novels written during the next fifty years (159). According to convention, the puzzle is mathematically stimulating, thereby engaging reader interest and inviting participation in solving the mystery. At its crux is the murder of Horatio Leavenworth, a millionaire business tycoon, whose body is found in the library of his home, with the door locked and the key missing. This is a whodunit of the locked-room variety popularized by Poe and Gaboriau. The suspects are members of the household who had access to the room. These include Mr. Leavenworth's two nieces, Mary and Eleanore; his private secretary, James Harwell, and the servants; however, the two nieces are the most likely suspects since they are heirs to the victim's considerable fortune. The structure of the Leavenworth murder puzzle is highly complex, based on inter-related sets of doubles: two murders (Horatio Leavenworth's and Hannah Chester's), two likely suspects (Mary and Eleanore Leavenworth), two sleuths (Ebenezer Gryce and Everett Raymond), and two settings (New York City and Saratoga Springs). Solving the puzzle, therefore, requires factoring out the discrepant elements by pursuing clues, evaluating evidence, and analyzing character.

Portraying the characters involves careful touches and controlled moments of revelation in order to keep the reader's attention, while not disclosing information that might lead to a premature unmasking of the murderer. The primary victim, Horatio Leavenworth, is a well-known and respected man who appeared not to have any enemies. According to convention, the victim is a shadowy figure, significant more in his relationships with other characters than in his individual role. As such his nieces, Mary and Eleanore, are focal: they are his only relatives, orphans whom he took into his home, and reputedly heirs to his fortune. Consequently, Mary and Eleanore Leavenworth are not only primary suspects but also front-page news. When a lawyer is called to assist the two young women, the reader is aware that legal as well as moral support may be needed. Mary is fair, delicate, innocent looking; Eleanore is dark, forceful, mysterious. Both of them are now potential victims of scandal mongers who could annihilate their reputations.

The young cousins became more than simply principal suspects, for Green portrayed them with depth and imagination. The characterizations of Mary and Eleanore captivated readers. Agatha Christie was to remark that the two women intrigued her when she first read the novel at the turn of the century (147). When Everett Raymond sees the two women for the first time, he sets the tone for the reader: "It was like a double vision of light and darkness that, while contrasting, neither assimilated nor harmonized" (143). Traditionally, light and darkness evoke associations of good and evil. Literary history reflects the motif of the "fair" and the "dark" lady—in the works of Petrarch, Shakespeare, Cooper, Hawthorne, Dickens, and Collins among others. In Fiedler's study of the American novel, he traces the mythic dimensions of the light and dark motif among literary heroines (206). The traditional treatment of the heroines reveals Green's cultural level as well as her ability to portray dynamic characters. It may also indicate that Green was influenced by what Fetterley calls "immasculation" (xx); that is, that writers (even female writers) tended to perpetuate a masculine view of women—in this case, the myth of the beautiful blonde and the intellectual brunette. Green's treatment of light and darkness, however, seems to build more on reader expectations than on her own convictions, for she goes on to create a reversal. In order to solve the puzzle, sleuth and reader alike must look beyond superficial physical traits to gain insight into the true character of each woman.

The social history embedded in the text exposes the stringent code imposed on young women. Along with the guilt or innocence of the heroines is the issue of their good names. Scandal will defile their reputations and, if not find them guilty of murder, it will mar their chances of marrying well. "The age of innocence," as Wharton was to call it,... "applied in particular to the young, girl, the debutante, whose single-minded purpose, her elders constantly reminded her, was to make a suitable marriage" (Lewis 35). As we shall see in Chapter Six, throughout her career Green focused on the problems of women—especially those endangered by greedy guardians or dishonest suitors. From the onset of the novel, the reader is warned that Mary and Eleanor are vulnerable: they are orphans and now, after the murder of their uncle, they are exposed to the wiles of the city and its perils. Their futures can only be made secure by "good" marriages. Tuttleton in *The Novel of Manners in America* emphasizes the predicament of the "marriageable girl" who must "have no past to conceal" (131). Thus Everett Raymond, the young lawyer retained to protect the women, articulates public sentiment when he bemoans the effect that scandal will have on the lives of these beautiful women.

While Everett Raymond operates in the capacity of amateur sleuth and assistant to police detective, Ebenezer Gryce, he never becomes a stooge or simply a sounding board for the official detective, nor does he exceed Gryce in his expertise. As such Raymond is not the kind of character Doyle developed ten years later in Watson. (However, it is possible that Doyle derived the concept of Watson from Green.) Raymond is emotionally involved in the case because of his infatuation with the two women. Mr. Gryce perceives his interest and manages to use it to gain the young man's cooperation. "Sometimes an uninitiated mind can intuitively discern the truth," Gryce tells Raymond (8). But he also explains that a police officer does not have the social advantage that a young, well educated man has among the upper echelon. As an outsider, Gryce does not have entree to the clubs and homes where Raymond is welcome. As narrator, Raymond has another important function: he is on intimate terms with his audience as he tells what he has seen and heard. This permits Mr. Gryce to pursue his investigation without revealing his own theories directly, effectively preventing the reader from having "unfair" access to elements of the puzzle.

Following the conventions of the genre, Green proceeds in a series of steps: an inquest determines that the victim has been murdered; the detective pursues all leads—examining evidence and interviewing witnesses; once the identity of the guilty party has been deduced, the detective sets up a confrontation drama to elicit a confession from the murderer. The rendering of scientific and procedural details is thorough and correct, giving the novel a realistic base not found in other American detection fiction—especially in works written by women. The inquest scenes present an accurate facsimile of procedures: jurymen (business men, no women were selected) are gathered from Fifth and Sixth Avenues; the city coroner presides; a medical expert testifies as does a representative of a firearms company; members of the household offer pertinent information. First the activities of the deceased on the evening of the murder are established. Then Dr. Maynard gives expert testimony on the victim's position and the path of the bullet: ". . . considering

the angle at which the bullet had entered the skull, it was evident
that the deceased must not only have been seated, but he must also
have been engaged in some occupation which drew his head forward.
For, in order that a ball should enter the head of a man sitting
erect at the angle seen here, of 45 degrees, it would be necessary
not only for the pistol to be held down, but in a peculiar
position...(16). A ballistics expert is then asked to determine if
Mr. Leavenworth's own gun might be the murder weapon. Upon
examination, he points out that although the barrel of the gun
has been wiped clean, a "faint line of smut on the edge of one
of the chambers" (51) indicates that it has recently been fired. The
disappearance of a maid, Hannah Chester, is noted; Mr. Gryce offers
the remains of a candle as evidence to show that she must have
left at night after the gaslights in the house had been turned off.
After all testimony is heard, the jury returns the verdict of murder
by person or persons unknown.

Once the charge is made, Gryce begins gathering evidence. (A
diagram of the murder scene is provided so that readers may match
wits with the detective.) Although he realizes that the coverup scheme
will make his task even more difficult, he takes up the challenge
and goes on to prove that he is eminently capable. Green does
not give Gryce a task that would not be comparable to those handled
by his literary predecessors. Critical to the case is the whereabouts
of Hannah Chester. Her trail leads to an unnamed resort town
upstate (most likely Saratoga Springs), but she is discovered too
late—the second victim in a cover-up murder made to look like
suicide. Again, the body is discovered in a locked room. Through
careful questioning, Gryce discovers that Hannah received a letter.
From this he deduces that a fake suicide note as well as some poison
was enclosed in the letter to the unwitting girl. The paper is tested
and found to contain particles of poison; then Gryce matches the
stationery with the stack from which it was taken in the Leavenworth
home. These procedures reflect the author's knowledge and her
concern for conveying a realistic account. They also help to define
Gryce's method—his use of forensic techniques, his persistence in

following through on deductive reasoning, his insight into human behavior.

Unmasking the murderer involves more than just the collection of evidence. Gryce proceeds step by step before making a last quantum leap into discovery. In locating the missing key to Mr. Leavenworth's room, he decides to look in an obvious place. (We can readily see the influence of Poe's "The Purloined Letter" in this touch.) He discovers the key entwined in the ornamental grillwork of an iron fireplace. When the Leavenworth cousins will not reveal their secret, he purports to arrest Eleanore, knowing that Mary will confess all if her cousin's honor is at stake: "The Most Beautiful Woman in New York under a Cloud" headlines the *Evening Post* (125). Mary reveals that one of them is secretly married and that each has been trying to protect the other. The plight of two orphaned women, even if one of them is a potential heiress, is a bid for the sympathy of readers.

In a confrontation drama, Ebenezer Gryce sets up a scene to force the guilty party to reveal himself. Raymond expresses his concern for Eleanore, but Gryce tells him that while everyone has been watching Eleanore, he has been looking at Mary. Through his secret pursuit of Mary, he has deduced who the murderer is. Much to the amazement of Raymond, Gryce shakes a confession out of the murderer by pretending to blame Mary for the crimes. Although Collins and Gaboriau had used the confrontation drama as a final stage in the detection process, neither author gave it specific religious significance. Green's treatment is not only moralistic, but reveals the application of Calvinistic doctrine. Gryce presides like a clergyman: his task is not only to elicit a confession from the murderer, but also to restore harmony—a state of grace to each of the characters. Thus Mary Leavenworth must do penance for all the pain she has caused if she is to be "restored." Solving the puzzle is not the only function of the detective. As W. H. Auden was to observe years later in his analysis of detective fiction, "the job of the detective is to restore the state of grace" (409).

Anna Katharine Green refined the detective novel, shaping its conventions and providing the link between Edgar Allan Poe and his American ancestors. Her works are significant not only for their contribution to detective fiction, but for their social history as well. And the fact that Green was a woman and virtually unknown when *The Leavenworth Case* was published makes her story all the more intriguing.

Chapter Two
The Shaping of a Writer

Others will enter the gates of the ferry
and cross from shore to shore,
Others will watch the run of the flood-tide,
Others will see the shipping of Manhattan
north and west,
and the heights of Brooklyn south and east,
Others will see the islands large and small
Fifty years hence, others will see them
as they cross, the sun half an hour high,
A hundred years hence, or ever so many
hundred years hence, others will see them
Will enjoy the sunset, the pouring-in
of the flood-tide,
the falling back to the sea of the ebb-tide.
—Walt Whitman from "Crossing Brooklyn Ferry"

Across the street from Brooklyn's Plymouth Church—a
landmark which was to mark her roots—Anna Catherine Green
was born on November 11, 1846. The daughter of Yankee parents,
she was to be a New Yorker all her life and an advocate of middle-
class morality. Her parents, James Wilson Green and Katherine
Ann Whitney Green, were of early New England stock with forebears
in Massachusetts and Connecticut.[1] Shortly before Anna's birth,
the Greens had moved from Manhattan to 59 Hicks Street, a narrow
clapboard house which they shared with relatives, the family of
Frederick Green.[2] Some months later they rented a house of their
own at 147 Adams Street. Although Anna spent only the first three

18

years of her life in Brooklyn (returning as an adult years later), a family pattern emerged during those early years which shaped her destiny.

Movement characterized the lifestyle of the family. James Wilson Green was different from other middle-class New England attorneys who established a law practice and stayed in a community to develop it. The birthplaces[3] of the Green children catalog the family's moves: Sarah Elizabeth was born on Catherine Street in Manhattan in 1833; James was born on Vanderwater Street also in Manhattan in 1835. Subsequently, the family moved to Richmond, Indiana where Sidney was born in 1843. By 1845, they were living in Manhattan again; and in 1846 they moved to Brooklyn.

A logical choice for a growing family, Brooklyn was spacious and possessed cultural and social advantages. Walt Whitman who was editing the *Brooklyn Eagle* from 1846-1848, described it as a desirable community, "hilly and elevated in its natural state—and these peculiarities...give us a sight unsurpassed and charming scenery...with much greater attractions for residences than our neighboring island of New York...a superior place for dwelling...hundreds and thousands of private dwellings for the comfort and luxury of the great body of middle class people" (*WW's NY* 56-57). The Heights, located on a bluff cross the river from the tip of Manhattan, had become an enclave of professional people, "Yankees and Yorkers of old American stock, Protestants who supported the four square churches" (Weld 9). It was a community where the Greens were likely to put down roots.

Brooklyn Heights attracted a large number of lawyers. Weld points out that in the Heights "there were many...Yankee lawyers, and Cranberry Street was hung thickly with their signs" (38). By 1855, according to United States Census figures, there were sixty-four lawyers practicing in Brooklyn. Although the Greens lived near Cranberry Street, James Wilson Green did not hang his shingle there; he had his office at 27 Fulton Street in Manhattan near the courthouse.[4] In his practice he represented clients before the Court of Common Pleas and also in United States Circuit Court.

A major feature of the Brooklyn community was Plymouth Church, a Presbyterian stronghold made famous by its pastor, Henry Ward Beecher. The son of the Reverend Lyman Beecher of Hartford, Connecticut, the younger Beecher started off as a frontier preacher in Indiana. He was called to Plymouth Church in 1847 on the strength of his father's reputation as well on his own merits. The Greens, who came from Presbyterian stock, joined Plymouth Church upon arrival in Brooklyn.[5] So great was their esteem for Beecher that their third son, born in 1849, was named Henry Ward Beecher Green. The elder Green maintained membership in the church for twenty years, even after he moved from the community. Anna was baptized in the church and remained a Presbyterian all her life. The values transmitted through the church were to become an integral part of her life and find expression in her writing.

If circumstances had been different, perhaps the Greens would have made a permanent home in Brooklyn. But a series of tragedies occurred between 1848 and 1849 which uprooted the family. In 1848, a huge conflagration destroyed half of the downtown area; in 1849 Plymouth Church burned to the ground and a cholera epidemic raged throughout the summer. At the end of the summer, Katherine Green died one month after giving birth to a son. The child died two weeks later. Anna, who was three years old at the time, was cared for from that time on by her sixteen-year old sister, Sarah, whom she called "mother-sister" (Interview: MAR). The loss of wife and mother brought the family even closer together and increased the hold that James Green would have over his children for years to come. Thus Anna was "protected" and well-cared for, but at the same time, she was also caught up in a tight family structure. She also developed a yearning to put down roots and make a home for herself.

After the deaths of his wife and infant son, James Green left Brooklyn and set up a series of temporary residences with family in Connecticut and Albany before settling in Buffalo, New York. In 1857, the Greens moved to a comfortable house at 50 Pearl Street in Buffalo. James Green had his law practice at 9 Harvey Block, becoming one of the fifteen attorneys in the city.[6] It was a city bursting with opportunity, a young city offering a marked contrast to Manhattan which was then experiencing financial panic. From its incorporation in 1832, Buffalo had grown from a frontier town to a metropolis with 81,000 residents. With the opening of the Erie Canal and the railroad linkage with New York City, Buffalo's iron, steel, and electrical power found ready markets. For Anna, the Buffalo years were very important. Her father had remarried, and "Mother Grace" brought a new dimension to the home. She even encouraged Anna's early attempts at writing. During this period Anna was attending public school, making friends, and establishing lasting communal ties. Thirty years later when she wanted security for her own young family, she and her husband returned to this city of her youth, built a home, and raised three children.

Perhaps the most remarkable and liberating feature of Anna Green's early life was her education. She was one of the handful of women of her generation to earn a college degree. In 1863, she enrolled at Ripley College in Poultney, Vermont—one of the few institutions in the nation to provide a college education to women— and the first institution to confer the degree in the state of Vermont. Here, Anna was encouraged to develop her literary interests. She became president of the Washington Irving Association—Irving's work was to influence her own presentation of the folklore and landscape of New York. It was also during this time that she set her sights upon becoming a poet, perceiving herself as a serious writer who would seek national recognition. When she graduated from college in June of 1866, Anna was one of six young women to receive the baccalaureate from Ripley College, and one of the few women college graduates in the country.[7]

After college, Anna returned home—as an unmarried woman she had few options. Despite the losses and changes in his life, her father remained the family patriarch, heading an extended family. When Anna's older brothers married, their wives joined the household. In the late 1860s the Greens resided in Haverstraw, New York; from there they moved to 12 Murray Street in Manhattan.

After her brother James died in 1876, his widow Annie remained with the family. When *The Leavenworth Case* was published, the entire family, including the wives of James and Sidney, were living at 543 Henry Street in Brooklyn Heights, very near the house where Anna was born. Sidney was working on Pearl Street in Manhattan; his father, then in his early seventies, was in semi-retirement. Sarah, the eldest, never married and lived at home also. (Eventually, she took up residence in a Brooklyn rooming house when her brother moved to East Orange, New Jersey.)[8]

Anna did not follow her sister's path. Even though she was living in the family home as an unmarried daughter, she sought a place for herself as a professional writer. In the years between graduation from college in 1866 and publication of her first novel in 1878, she struggled for identity as a writer. Although her father approved of her writing poetry—a genteel form, appropriate for a woman, he was not receptive to fiction. Consequently, when Anna decided to write a novel, she wrote in secret, taking only her step-mother into her confidence ("Noted Buffalonians" 1). For over six years, she filled school notebooks with her story. When the manuscript was finished, she presented it to her father—after reading half of it, he conceded that she had produced something worthwhile. Publication of the story, however, was another hurdle. As an unknown writer and a woman, Anna was not in a position to bargain. Fortunately, through her father's connections, she was introduced to critic Rossiter Johnson who recommended the manuscript to George Putnam. In her quiet way, Anna was tenacious and daring in risking the ire of her father; she was also practical in gaining his support for her work.

The Leavenworth Case launched Anna's career, and she was determined to make the most of her success. As a first step in assuming a professional image, Anna changed her middle name to "Katharine." She accepted increased social invitations and made contacts with the literary establishment. Her first novel became a best-seller in the United States and received equal attention abroad. The detective novel was enjoying huge popularity in Europe, largely through the efforts of masters like Gaboriau and Collins. Thus the manner of Green's entrance into the field was timely. After *The Leavenworth Case*, three more successful novels followed: *A Strange Disappearance* (1880), *XYZ* (1883), and *Hand and Ring* (1883). With fame came the recognition that enabled her to bring her poetry to the public. In 1882, George Putnam agreed to publish *The Defense of the Bride*, a slim volume containing twenty-six poems representing her earliest literary efforts. As we shall see in Chapter Three, these lyrics offer some insight into Green's character and provide a link to her fiction.

Even more surprising than her accomplishments in detective fiction were Anna's courtship and marriage to Charles Rohlfs, a struggling young actor. At the time, Anna was thirty-seven years old—in fact, old enough to be considered a "spinster." It was not the typical "match" for someone of her social class. Charles Rohlfs was eight years her junior and the son of German immigrants, Fredericke Hunte and Peter Rohlfs. However, after being "properly introduced" by the pastor of South Congregational Church, the Reverend Albert Lyman, Rohlfs courted the then well-known, Miss Green ("Noted Buffalonians" 1). The Rohlfs family belonged to South Congregational Church, located in a working-class neighborhood south of Prospect Park, home to both German and Irish immigrants. Undoubtedly Rohlfs' religious affiliation was a crucial factor in gaining the approval of Anna's father.

Charles Rohlfs was a tall, imposing man with a dynamic voice— quite different from the diminutive and unassuming Anna. He made his stage debut in Boston in 1868 in "The Exiles," produced at the Boston Theatre. From then on, he took a series of small parts, often traveling from city to city. At the Criterion Theatre in Manhattan, he had the opportunity to play opposite Booth—a milestone in his early career. But Anna was much more famous than he; later he commented that he felt like he had married *The Leavenworth Case*—so popular was the novel at the time ("Noted Buffalonians" 1). Charles Rohlfs was clearly less known than his bride: in fact, their wedding announcement in the *Brooklyn Eagle* identified him as "Mr. Rholse" ("Rholse-Green," 15). They were married on November 25, 1884 at South Congregational Church; James Wilson Green, then seventy-five years old gave his daughter away. A small reception was held at the home of friends on Union Street.

As a condition of their marriage, Charles Rohlfs was to give up his acting career. This was Anna's father's decision and, true to his promise, Rohlfs did leave the theater—at least for a time. He returned to an art that he had studied at Cooper Union, the design and crafting of iron stoves. For a short time, the couple lived in Taunton, Connecticut where he plied his trade. Then they returned to Brooklyn and took up residence at 302 Fourth Street in the South Park district, not in the more prestigious Heights. Although Anna was enjoying a measure of literary fame, they lived simply and quietly as they pursued their careers, each encouraging the other to succeed.

After six years Charles Rohlfs returned to the stage to appear in a dramatized version of *The Leavenworth Case*. Perhaps the demise of James Wilson Green freed Rohlfs of his commitment, or perhaps his love of the theatre simply prevailed. Anna's position on her husband's acting career is expressed best in her novel *The Sword of Damocles* (1909). The novel, which is dedicated to her father, opens with a young "performer," concert pianist Bertram Mandeville, promising his future father-in-law that he will give up his career: "Three weeks ago I was satisfied with my profession, if not enthusiastic over it, today I ask nothing but to be allowed to enter upon some business that in three years' time will place me where I can be the fit mate of any woman in this land..." (8). The young woman is distressed by her father's demands but dares not reproach him. Even though she was initially attracted to her lover by his "art," she finds herself accomplice to her father's demands, for a father "has a right to expect both wealth and position in a son-in-law" (9). The parallels between the fictional couple's circumstances and that of Anna Green and Charles Rohlfs are apparent. As we shall see in Chapter 6, Miss Green voiced in her fiction her rejection of tyrannical fathers and her support for women caught up in unfair courtships or marriages. As patriarch of the family, James Green maintained firm control over his children. Anna was used to acceding to her father's wishes; she never openly challenged to his authority, but in her quiet way, she was able to circumvent barriers and pursue her own goals.

While Anna single-mindedly pursued a career as a writer, Charles Rohlfs changed careers. He had moved from designing iron stoves to making furniture in the 1890s. After the dramatization of *The Leavenworth Case* in 1891, his yearning to act was rekindled. Letters to Augustin Daly reveal that in the spring of 1896, Rohlfs was appearing in Boston in Moliere's *The Physician In Spite of Himself,* and in *The Merchant of Venice.* In April of 1896, he wrote to Daly requesting an audition; in September he tried again: "I am very desirous to secure an engagement under your direction to play character comedy parts. Will you kindly look at the accompanying photographs. All but two are meant for Squanarelle in Moliere's *The Physician in Spite of Himself.* They may give you an idea as to my probable fitness for this line of dramatic work" (Letters: CR-AD). Daly apparently did not have an opening for Rohlfs, but the fact that Rohlfs was aggressively seeking roles and was willing to travel, as the Boston engagement indicates, shows that he was still seeking a place for himself in the theater.

Dramatizing *The Leavenworth Case* in 1891 was a joint venture for husband and wife which brought mutual enjoyment as well as income. This was not Anna's first play; she had been interested in the theater long before she met Charles Rohlfs. A decade earlier, on August 30, 1876, she had written to Augustin Daly, then manager and director of the Fifth Avenue Theater, asking him to consider the manuscript of a play that she had enclosed for possible production at his theater (Letters: AKG-AD). Her connection with Augustin Daly was facilitated by his brother, Joseph Daly, who was a Judge in the New York City Court of Common Pleas and a friend of her father. (Judge Daly and his first wife Emma were among the guests at Anna's wedding.) She contacted Augustin Daly on several occasions about the possibility of dramatizing her novels (Daly 444). By 1890 Daly managed a chain of theaters in New York and London; both he and his brother adapted classic literary works as well as contemporary novels for stage production. Green was among a host of other writers of fiction, including Wilkie Collins, who approached Daly about adapting their novels for the theater (Daly 444). Neither Green nor Collins succeeded in convincing Daly to produce their works.

After her marriage, Anna proclaimed on title pages of her works her new identity, "Mrs. Charles Rohlfs." Two children were born to her while she lived in Brooklyn: Rosamund in 1885 and Sterling in 1887. Motherhood apparently did not deter her from proceeding with her career, but she was also motivated by continuing financial needs. During this period she wrote three novels: *The Mill Mystery* (1886), *7 to 12* (1887), and *Behind Closed Doors* (1888), as well as short stories for the periodical market. As their family grew, financial considerations and business opportunities led the Rohlfs to Buffalo. Charles' skill at furniture-making was developing, but Anna's income from her writing was still their major resource. At this time they were helping to support Anna's older sister Sarah who was living alone in Brooklyn. Sarah took in sewing, but she could not meet all her needs and required the assistance that came from both Anna and her brother Sidney.[9] Charles' mother, Fredericke Rohlfs, whom he helped to support, died in 1888—it was after her death that Charles and Anna moved to Buffalo. They rented a house at 26 Highland Avenue. If the move was at first a trial to see how they would fare, when they bought property in 1890 bordering the large city park at the center of the city, they had determined to stay.[10]

The early Buffalo years reflect a settling-in to the community. Anna continued her writing, while Charles set up his furniture studio. They joined the First Presbyterian Church where Charles served as an elder and Anna became active on volunteer committees. Buffalo had been home to Anna in her youth, and it was a city where she still had friends. She seized the opportunity to improve the quality of life for her growing family: the cost of living was less than it had been in Brooklyn and land was cheaper. After a third child, Roland, was born in 1892, the Rohlfs acquired a live-in housekeeper, Mrs. Biegh, to release Anna during the day so that she could write (Interview: MAR).

The Rohlfs' lifestyle was unusual by local standards: their home was different and the creative interests of both husband and wife were extraordinary. Their house at 156 Park Street, a tudor style dwelling, was designed by Charles Rohlfs especially for his own family. With its distinctive design and its mission style furniture, their home was unlike any other in the city. Rohlfs designed special functional additions, such as an enclosed space beneath a side porch to garage his youngest son's motorcycle (Interview: MAR). On the surface, Charles Rohlfs was an ordinary man—a craftsman and small businessman, but at the same time he was an actor, taking roles in plays whenever he could. Anna, to all outward appearances, was a "housewife." She kept house with minimal help, raised her children, tended her garden, and served on church committees. Typically, she could be observed in a high-necked Victorian dress weeding her garden, accompanied by one or two pet cats. But there was another side to her—a quiet, creative dimension which people rarely saw. A disciplined writer, she worked every day at her profession—it was her first priority, never an avocation.

The period between their marriage in 1884 and the turn of the century, was a period of affirmation for Anna and Charles Rohlfs. Anna's income from her fiction was providing enough money for them to travel. Their trip to Europe in 1890 was the first and only time they went abroad; it was memorable in its pleasures as well as in the contacts that developed for both of them. Anna was welcomed by the British who were ardent fans of detective fiction. Among the more prominent who were readers and acquaintances of Green were classics professor A.V. Dicey of Oxford University, literary critic Walter Besant, and future prime minister Stanley Baldwin (Letters: AKG). Charles Rohlfs met British craftsmen who welcomed him and later nominated him for membership in the Royal Society of Arts of London.

Thus by the 1890s Charles Rohlfs—actor, iron master, inventor—succeeded as a designer of furniture. He got his start by making pieces for their own home, after finding quality furniture too expensive. A man of definite tastes, Rohlfs developed his own style. According to Robert Clark in *The Arts and Crafts Movement in America*, "By 1890 Rohlfs was making plain oak pieces with unusual details, which had many characteristics in common with the style later known as Mission" (28). One of the first tasks he accomplished was the design and execution of a writing chair for his wife—a large oak piece with a wide, contoured right arm to accommodate her notebook. From the success of the furniture made for his own home, Rohlfs was encouraged to set up a small business. His studio was more like an artist's workshop; Rohlfs considered each piece an individual creation and demanded excellence of himself and the artisans who worked for him. An early vignette of Charles Rohlfs described his working style: "He draws his designs. A workman will turn out a small model. He will study this for some time, make improvements, useful and artistic, make another design and have another model made.... But when that chair or whatever else it may be,...is made, it is perfection. It is more than that, it is that rare combination of utility and art" ("A Little Known Husband" 1291). He displayed his furniture at the Pan American Exposition held in Buffalo in 1901, his stall located near the prestigious Tiffany craftsmen. Ultimately, Charles Rohlfs was to receive international recognition as a furniture designer. Today his work can be viewed at the Princeton Museum and at the Metropolitan Museum of Art in New York.

While Charles Rohlfs worked at his craft, Anna wrote continuously. During the 1890s she published an astounding number of novels and novelets, including *The Forsaken Inn* (1890), *A Matter of Millions* (1891), *Cynthia Wakeham's Money* (1892), *Marked Personal* (1893), *Miss Hurd—An Enigma* (1894), *Dr. Izard* (1895), *The Doctor, His Wife, and the Clock* (1895), *That Affair*

Next Door (1987). *Lost Man's Lane* (1898), *Agatha Webb* (1899). Along with the novels, she was also writing short stories, which appeared in periodical form and then were later collected into an edition entitled *The Old Stone House and Other Stories* (1891). As an examination of her works will show, Green was not only trying out new genres during this period; she was also developing alternative styles. While the detective novel was still her claim to fame, she tried her hand at romance and focused on social issues as well as on the pure mystery puzzle.

Anna also developed a lively correspondence with notable individuals. Among them were Mary Wilkins Freeman and Arthur Conan Doyle (Letters: MWF-AKG 6/25/95; ACD-AKG 11/16/94, 11/27/94). During his tour of the United States in 1894, Doyle arranged to meet Anna in Buffalo. At that time her place in detective fiction was well established, while Doyle was a relative newcomer. Through her literary agent, Galbraith Welch Dwyer, Anna maintained contacts with publishers and received requests for her stories from editors of periodicals, among them Edward Bok (Letters: EB-AKG 6/24/03). Although she had loyal fans and was assured of a market for her work, Anna was not part of any literary group or clique. She was essentially an independent thinker and a shy, introverted person who put her energies into her work and her family.

Anna and Charles Rohlfs were also caring parents who encouraged their children to discover their own talents. They expected their sons to pursue challenging careers, "to seek their fortune," and were proud of their achievements (Interview: MAR). Sterling and Roland, were in the vanguard of aviation, training as pilots at the Curtiss Flying School in upstate New York. Sterling settled in New Mexico, married and fathered two daughters. Roland married and eventually made his home on Long Island, often flying on special trips for the Roosevelts at Oyster Bay. All seemed to prosper until the tragic death of Sterling Rohlfs—killed piloting a plane that crashed at Toluca, Mexico in 1928, an event which received national publicity because the passengers included representatives of President Calles of Mexico and General Obregon. Obregon who was a target for assassination was not present. U.S. officials including former U.S. Ambassador Morrow attended Sterling Rohlfs' funeral. Although the *New York Times* reported the "real cause a mystery" (10), some observers thought that Rohlfs and his passengers may well have been on a secret mission for the United States government when his plane went down, by accident or sabotage. Years later Charles Rohlfs lamented, "...we never did know just what happened there...." ("Noted Buffalonians" 2). That tragedy was succeeded in 1930 by the death of their only daughter, Rosamund.

By the turn of the century, Green still maintained a loyal following of readers although her popularity had begun to wane. To a new generation, her style was heavy compared with that of rising authors like Mary Roberts Rinehart whose language was plain and less burdened with cautionary messages. Yet Green did not stop writing—her imagination was still fertile. Between 1900 and 1923, she produced *The Circular Study* (1900), *One of My Sons* (1901), *The Filigree Ball* (1903), *The Millionaire Baby* (1905), *The House in the Mist* (1905), *The Amethyst Box* (1905) *The Woman in the Alcove* (1906), *The Chief Legatee* (1907), *The Mayor's Wife* (1907), *The Sword of Damocles* (1909), *Three Thousand Dollars* (1910), *The House of the Whispering Pines* (1910) *Initials Only* (1911), *Dark Hollow* (1914), *To the Minute, Scarlet and Black* (1916), *Mystery of the Hasty Arrow* (1917), and *The Step on the Stair* (1923). Her career was long and fruitful. As we shall see in the following chapters, her works offer the modern reader an opportunity to study the development of detective fiction, to appreciate the efforts of an American woman in her struggle to achieve recognition, and to survey the panorama of American social life at the turn of the century.

Chapter Three
Choices

Though Anna Katharine Green is best known for her classic detective fiction, she also tried her hand at other forms of literature, including poetry and drama. These lesser known works provide insight to her professional development and to the opportunities available for women writers. Poetry was her first love: she had aspired to be a poet from girlhood. Detective fiction was her second choice. When she could not find a publisher for her poetry, she looked for a genre that had wide appeal. Sensing the pulse of the times, she put her efforts into detective fiction at a time when it was becoming increasingly popular, winning almost instant fame with the publication of *The Leavenworth Case*. Not content to turn out formulaic prose, she developed variations of the detective novel and also wrote novelets, short stories, and plays. For the modern reader, the choices she made as a writer and the scope of her works offer evidence of Green's motivation, versatility, and achievement.

Poetry

The Defence of the Bride (1882) represents Green's early poetry. A slim volume (124 pages), it is a collection of twenty-six poems dating in composition from 1871 and possibly earlier. Within the volume are some of the poems that she sent to Ralph Waldo Emerson in 1868 for evaluation. At the time, it was not easy for any poet, especially a woman poet, to find a publisher. As Gilbert and Gubar point out, when Rufus Griswold edited the nineteenth century anthology entitled *The Female Poets of America*, he "outlined a theory of literary sex roles which builds upon, and clarifies,...implications of the metaphor of literary paternity. [According to Griswold,] it is less easy to be assured of the genuineness of literary ability in women than in men" (9). Consequently, when Green wrote to Emerson, she was hoping he would remember meeting her at Ripley College and would give her the support she so desperately needed for publication. His letter of response is cordial but not enthusiastic.

Concord
June 30, 1868

Dear Miss Green,

   ...(The poems) are well chosen & give me as you meant they should a good guess at your style & quality of your work: "they clearly indicate a good degree attained in power of expression, & the specimens together show the variety and range of the thought. I think one is to be congratulated on every degree of success in this kind, because it opens a new world of resource & to which every experience glad or sad contributes new means and occasion. But it is quite another question whether it is to be made a profession,—whether one may dare leave all other things behind, & write...(Emerson, 22-23).

The "question" as to whether or not writing poetry "is to be made a profession" implies that Emerson did not feel that Green should "dare leave all other things behind" and pursue a career as a poet. If Emerson had been impressed by Green's poems, he would have encouraged her to seek publication. For a woman who wrote poetry to gain entree to the inner circle of recognized poets, she needed the protection of a male sponsor. As Cheryl Walker points out in her study of women poets before 1900, the male publishing establishment did not consider the poetry of women according to the same standards applied to that of men. She notes, "...Griswold's final separation of male and female poets places only men in *The Poets and Poetry of America*. Women were relegated to a separate volume: *The Female Poets of America*" (56). Even then, to have her work accepted for publication a woman had to have the right connections. A case in point is a contemporary of

Green, Helen Hunt Jackson, who gained recognition as a poet only after "seeking out the friendship of T. W. Higginson" (Walker 95).

Though Green's poetry did not receive critical acclaim, the poems survive. George Putnam published her small volume, probably as a courtesy, following the success of her detective fiction. But the poems are significant both in themselves and in what they reveal about the author. The more personal lyrics are as good, I suggest, as those of her female contemporaries (like Lucy Larcom or Helen Hunt Jackson).

"The Defence of the Bride," the first poem in the collection, is the kind of poem male poets had been writing—Green successfully emulated the *male* tradition. Written in the heroic style, the poem is a narrative of love and honor set in medieval France. According to the narrative, Sir Beaufort leaves his castle and young bride under the protection of the sons of Saint Germain. After giving allegiance to their lord, the young men fight the enemy, losing their own lives so that "not a shadow of dishonor has so much as touched her head" (8). Only the youngest, Enguerrand, who has slain "twenty foreman of her honor" (8) remains alive when Sir Beaufort returns to rout the enemy. However, Enguerrand confesses that "While the others fought for honor, I by passion was made strong" (9). Honorable to the end, Enguerrand admits his love for the lady, but proudly asserts that though his heart has strayed, his "hand has e'er been loyal" (9). Both in form and content, the poem reflects the style of nineteenth century male romantic poets such as Scott, Tennyson, and Longfellow. Seven more poems follow in a similar style with French heroic motifs.

The major limitation of the heroic poems is their imitative style. Green had not been to France; the use of French tradition reflects her reading, but not her experience. And the voice in the poems is a *male* voice. We can see in these poems the cultural pressure to use the authoritative male voice. Ironically, the use of that voice may have influenced publishers against accepting her poetry. As Cheryl Walker points out, publishers expected women to write feminine poems, noting that "the *North American Review* praised Lydia Sigourney for *lacking* the ambition to attempt the highest level of poetry;...hers was 'true feminine genius' " (Walker 55).

A more authentic voice is heard in Green's simple lyrics focusing on themes of separation and loss. In most of these poems she speaks with the poetic "I"—with the voice of a woman. "Separated," for example, shows how the speaker copes with being separated temporarily from her loved one:

> I know not how, but from the surging sea
> Of these thy thoughts, some echo comes to me,
> Moving my soul till from its billow rise
> The answering strain for which they spirit cries,
> And then, or joy, or sorrow holds the throne
> Of thy strong heart, thou art no more alone (102).

Since the speaker feels that communication is still possible even though she and her lover are not together, the sense of loss is not as intense as it is in other poems. "In Farewell" presents a philosophical view of the break-up of a relationship:

> I met thee, dear, and loved thee—yet we part,
> Thou on thine unknown way and I on mine,
> Ere the music of my woman's heart.
> Has had full time to harmonize with thine (66).

Not having had "full time" together, the speaker seems resigned rather than upset that they parted when their lives took different directions. "The music of my woman's heart" seems to reinforce the distinction here between what a woman feels and what a man might feel in a relationship. In each of these poems the tone is positive, not accusatory or despairing. But in the majority of poems the sense of loss dominates and the speaker assumes the role of the "wronged woman."

The recurring theme in the poems suggests that Green was preoccupied with separation. Typically, the speaker is a female who expresses her dejection at the end of a romantic relationship. She is depicted as innocent and vulnerable, while the male is materialistic and easily influenced by opportunities to make a more profitable match. Although the Civil War provoked a nation-wide sensitivity to loss, Anna may well have experienced a personal loss. Considering the fact that she did not marry until age thirty-eight, late for a woman of her generation, she herself may have had an unsuccessful relationship.

In "Through the Trees" the speaker describes how she feels when she sees her former lover with another woman:

> If I had known his deep love
> Could make her face so fair to see;
> If I had known her shy and I
> Could make him stoop so tenderly
> I had not come; I had not come (9).

Regret dominates this poem, indicating that the speaker is deeply hurt by the discovery of her lover's inconstancy. Another poem, "Three Letters," presents the point of view of the fickle lover: "Sweet, when I gave my troth to you/ I loved you—or imagined so;/ But winds may change..." (37). Although the lover is able to rationalize his change of heart and dismiss any misgivings about his former commitment, the jilted woman grieves. "In Light: In Dark" expresses her lament:

> Gloom hath with her no part,
> While in his sight her soul greatens and glows
> ...I clasp the cross and cry
> Strength, Holy Rood! (36).

The crucifixion imagery projects the speaker's intense suffering at the betrayal of her love.

The effects of separation are also the focus of a series of narrative portraits: "Isabel Maynor," "Paul Isham," "Rosa, Dying," and "Myrna." More than in any other poems in the collection, these reflect the beginnings of the prose narratives Green was to produce later. Isabel Maynor, for example, could easily be the prototype for the scores of "wronged women" whom Green characterized in her fiction. Pledged to Philip Lee, whom she has not seen in years, Isabel turns down other suitors in the vain hope that Philip will return and be true to his promise. The speaker of the poem laments Lee's treachery, while Lee puts the blame on "moneyed men, the world, and its abuse" (86). As her fiction reveals, Green viewed greed as the basis for much of society's aberrant behavior.

A reviewer for *Harper's* comments on the strength of Green's narrative poems: "She has the true story-teller's facility for investing what she has to say with interest, and for keeping expectation on the stretch, and she delivers her message with masculine force and brevity."[1] The "masculine force" is an interesting term, which perhaps says more of the reviewer than the poet, but there is "force" in the poems—at times unadorned and powerful in its thrust. Green excels in the plain style; she is less successful when her voice is obscured in the romantic, longer poems recounting historical deeds of cultures other than her own. Green's poetry, like her fiction, is best when her own voice is heard.

Drama

Green's poetic drama, *Risifi's Daughter* (1887), contains some of the same themes as her poems—greed, love, and honor. A five act classical tragedy set in Renaissance Italy, the drama focuses on a marriage arranged between Giovanni, a Florentine prince, and Ginevra, the daughter of a wealthy merchant. Although he questions whether it is honorable to marry for money to bolster his family's declining fortune, Giovanni agrees to marry Ginevra after his father exhorts him: "But gold brings power,/ And power brings honor" (14). Giovanni is also assured of Ginevra's virtue: "Virtue, Prince,/ Doth need no pedigree to make it lovely" (11). However, conflict arises when it is revealed that Camillo, Giovanni's younger brother, and Ginevra are in love and had hoped to marry. Though Giovanni is willing to renounce his claim to Ginevra, her father refuses because only the elder son bears the princely title: "I'd have her princess,/ And princess shall she be, or die a maid" (97). The conflict is resolved when Giovanni commits suicide in order to make his younger brother heir to his title and thus worthy of marriage to Ginevra.

Risifi's Daughter is a period piece that reflects Green's level of education as well as her craftsmanship. Like her poetry, the style emulates that of nineteenth century male authors, such as Shelley in *The Cenci.* On this basis alone, I suggest that her work would not have been readily accepted by publishers, given their expectations of female poets. A revisionist reading of Green's poetry and poetic drama, however, reveals her to be under-rated and overlooked, like many other competent women writers of her generation.

Despite the faint praise for her poetry and drama, Green was determined to make herself heard, to test her voice in a range of genres. She had a genuine love of theatre and continued to write plays even though *Risifi's Daughter* did not bring acclaim. The only play that was staged was *The Leavenworth Case,* adapted for the theatre by Basil Ring (pseudonym for Wilbur Braun) as a drama in three acts. It was produced in Chicago in the fall of 1891. A *New York Times* critic acknowledged the success of the novel but perceived the play as "too weird to be immensely popular" (*NYT* 13). The popularity of the novel, however, ensured an enthusiastic audience and with Charles Rohlfs cast in the role of the murderer, the production capitalized on public interest in the husband and wife duo.

As her letters to Broadway producer Augustin Daly indicate, Green wrote plays and continued to seek producers for them.[2] She sent the following letter to Augustin Daly dated August 13, 1894:

Dear Mr. Daly:
      I send you by Express today—charges paid—lbs. of ms. plays.

My dramatization of "The Leavenworth Case" was sufficiently successful to tempt me to try again. The plays sent you are the very latest efforts in play making.

Will you do me the kindness to look them over or have some competent person read them that I may be assured whether or not it is advisable for me to make any further efforts in the line of play writing.

Of course, if you should find them suitable to your requirements I should be highly gratified.

AKGR

The "lbs. of ms. plays" indicates the quantity of material that Green produced. Daly did not produce any of her plays, but the letter reflects a persistence to be heard, to seek a competent reading of her work.

Short Fiction

Although Green did not limit herself to writing fiction, this was her area of success. Publishers of popular literature were much more responsive to public taste; sales depended more on what the masses found to their liking rather than upon the judgment of an elite group—such as the readers and publishers of poetry. *The Leavenworth Case* was so popular that by the time Green's short stories and novelets appeared in magazines, she was internationally known. As millions of readers subscribed to popular magazines, the periodical market developed, and Green found a ready outlet for her stories. This market provided a place for both the short story and the novelete as well as a quick return for the author. Murch points out that "the magazine reading multitudes of the 1890s preferred short stories" to "the full-length detective novel" (164).

Green responded to the demand: between 1885 and 1900, she wrote most of her shorter fiction. Individual stories appeared in periodicals and then were collected and published in hardback editions; novels were also serialized before appearing in single editions. The practice of publishing on two fronts was both profitable and common to popular writers of the time. But personal considerations may also have motivated Green, for this was a time in her life when money was scarce. Her husband's business was not lucrative. Consequently, although they owned land, it was not until 1900 that Charles and Anna finally built their own house. Even then, they lived conservatively, without extensive financial assets.

The Novelete

Green's novelets are not as well-crafted as her short stories, for the brevity of the novelet made a significant difference to Green. The form posed structural problems, providing neither the scope of the novel nor the compactness of the short story. Perhaps Green handled the form as well as any of her contemporaries. The fact that the novelet died out is an obvious comment on its limitations. But clearly, it did not offer Green the broad canvas she needed for the intricacies of circumstance and character, the twists and turns which her mathematical mind developed so well. As in her novels, she succeeds when she provides an unusual but reasonable puzzle and sufficient development of character to add a psychological dimension to her story. Her novelets include *Three Thousand Dollars, The Old Stone House, 7 to 12, One Hour More, XYZ, The Doctor His Wife and the Clock, Market Personal, The Forsaken Inn,* and *The House of the Whispering Pines.* Each of these works focuses on a crime and its solution, but the plots do not seem to adapt well to the novelet form—they are either too flimsy or too complex. The following analysis of selected novelets reflect both weaknesses and strengths in Green's handling of the form.

7 to 12 and *One Hour More* (1887), two novelets published together in a single volume, are mediocre stories. *7 to 12* is a version of a well-worn plot found in European and American fiction—the search for the missing jewels. The plot involves a New York City matron who reports her valuable pearls lost. Mrs. Winchester is portrayed as a snob, concerned more about her property than about her son who marries a loving but penniless girl. (The sub-plot of the young couple's romance evokes the "Cinderella" motif which nineteenth century readers found especially appealing.) When her husband disappears, "leaving debts of an enormous nature behind him and no assets wherewith to pay those debts" (78), he reveals his guilt. But the story does not end here: Mrs. Winchester's character is still at issue. Thus the reader learns that she "whose pride was perhaps phenomenal in its way, never recovered from the shock thus given her;...(now) a depressed and humiliated woman," she is taken in by the son and daughter-in-law she once rejected (78). The moral not only tends to be pedantic and detracts from the puzzle, but it delays the narrative.

The second story, *One Hour More*, is imitative and possesses neither the resilience of Green's ethnic American stories nor the challenge of a puzzle. This story takes place in France. Two brothers have fallen in love with the same girl; one goes off to escape punishment for embezzlement, while the other labors to pay off his brother's debt. Elise, unfortunately, loves the errant brother. When Jean asks her to marry him, he realizes she is not in love with him: "I do not expect you to love me just yet, but you need a protector; let me be that protector" (109). Elise marries Jean, but she does not acknowledge the love that she has developed for him and despairs when he dies before she has the chance to tell him. Basically, the story is a romance, not a mystery, and lacks the puzzle that Green's more engaging stories present. As a novelete, it is a belabored story—perhaps compressed as a short story it might have been more energetic.

While Green's least successful novelets are usually highly romanticized versions of worn motifs, her most successful are realistic and contain a conundrum that is a challenge for the reader. *Three Thousand Dollars*, a thin account of theft with a Cinderella ending, is one of her least successful. The heroine is a trusted female bank employee who is the only person entrusted with the means to open the bank's safe. This is accomplished by singing an aria: the frequency of the lock is tuned to her voice. Unusual as this device may be, Green burdens the story with cliches and romantic trappings, including a poor, but honorable, suitor. Novelets were particularly in demand for women's magazines; thus Green may have written this story and other highly romantic novelets expressly for the women's market.

A better story is *The Doctor, His Wife and the Clock*—this novelet is longer, more complex and tougher. Although a murder puzzle, it focuses on the effects of the crime upon the assailant. A psychological study of guilt, it engages the reader not only in solving the puzzle, but also in understanding the pathology of guilt. The depth and originality of this work render it superior to most of her other novelets.

The Short Story

In contrast to the novelet, the short story offered a well-defined medium for Green—a single focus, a more concise plot. From the legacy of Edgar Allan Poe who developed the mystery short story, writers who followed inherited a stylized form. In order to convey a sense of Green's success with the short story, I have selected a range of stories for examination which reveal her limitations as well as her versatility, imagination, and craftsmanship.

Among the short stories which contain unusual devices is "The Little Steel Coils," which focuses on a strange package sent to a man on the day of his sudden death—a package containing steel coils. Prior to her husband's death, his wife had received in the mail a printed notice of his death. Suspecting foul play, she employs a private detective to investigate the circumstances of her husband's death. Early on, the detective discovers that one of the coils has a sharp edge covered with a rare poison, thus deducing that the unfortunate husband cut his hand on the coil and assimilated the poison. However, "The Little Steel Coils" is not a "how-dunnit," relying solely on deducing the effect of the steel coils—it is a psychological study which pits the intelligence of the detective against that of the killer. What kind of person chooses this method of murder? And how can the detective prove murder and achieve justice? Green successfully takes the reader through the stages leading to the resolution of the crime.

"The Bronze Hand" also centers on a deadly device—a sculpted bronze hand. The figure, located in the waiting room of a doctor's office, covertly functions as an electric signalling device triggered by a ring placed on the hand. Operating like a telegraph system, the signal conveys the execution orders of targeted government leaders. Green usually steers clear of politics, but she creates tension by building upon the threat of anarchy without actually naming the group responsible for undermining the government. While stories with a mechanical center might not appeal to everyone, they have merit. Although brief and dependent upon a gimmick, these stories are more unified and aesthetically pleasing than other Green stories that ramble, taking turns that a novel could sustain but which de-energize the short story.

"Room #3" is an example of a story with a basically good plot that rambles and lacks control. A woman reports that her mother has died under suspicious circumstances at the Three Forks Inn— an isolated roadhouse. Her credibility is questioned, however, when she insists that the room where her mother stayed was papered with pink floral wallpaper. Room #3 is covered with faded blue paper which is old and appears to have been on the walls for years. After a young detective discovers how the innkeepers made the "switch," the story takes a curve into escapades with highwaymen and the romance of the detective and the bereaved daughter. It takes a fire to bring the culprits (and the plot) under control.

In contrast, "Midnight in Beauchamp Row" is one of Green's most successful stories. It combines atmosphere, the puzzle, and a realistic female persona—features which Green develops well. Letty Chivers, a young bride at home alone on Christmas Eve, has been left guardian of $2000—her husband's company payroll. Ned Chivers has hidden the money in the house after being called away on business. Basically, the plot is simple, but Green creates an appealing atmosphere and provides credible twists to toughen the mystery. As we have noted in her novels, Green is facile at presenting rural as well as city backgrounds. She evokes the natural isolation of the upper reaches of Westchester County (Washington Irving territory) where the Chivers' modest cottage is located. "It was the last house in Beauchamp Row, and it stood several rods away from its nearest neighbor. It was a pretty house in the daytime, but owing to its deep, sloping roof and small bediamoned windows it had a lonesome look at night, not withstanding the crimson hall-light which shone through the leaves of its vine-covered doorway" (3). Not only is the spot lonely, but snow is falling.

Letty Chivers has the spirit of a frontier wife who uses her wits to survive. Assuming responsibility for keeping the money secure, she moves it to a less obvious place. And even though she fears for her safety, she admits two bedraggled wayfarers seeking shelter from the blustery storm. A play on the doubles motif is apparent in the characterization of the two strangers: the first is a drunken tramp who terrorizes her before the second man—a Negro—arrives. Letty is not actually raped or abused, but the threat of abuse is there. The tramp toys with her unspoken fears: " 'Ugh! ugh! But it is warm here!' he cried, his nostrils dilating with animal-like enjoyment, that itself was repugnant to her feminine delicacy. 'Do you know, missus, I shall have to stay here all night? Can't go out in that gale again; not such a fool.' Then with a sly look at her trembling form and white face he insinuatingly added, 'All alone, missus?' " (11). The intruders strike at the fears of female readers who were accustomed to real-life accounts of violence detailed in the daily tabloids. The ending is a surprise: the would-be thief is felled and unmasked by the second wayfarer. The disclosure of the identity of the thief provides a dramatic and aesthetically satisfying denouement. Green does not "add on" cautionary messages, nor does she arrange a happy ending. Thus the story retains its integrity.

Green's most famous story is "Staircase at Heart's Delight," published in 1890, recounting the beginnings of her serial detective Ebenezer Gryce. The story recalls Manhattan's past—a romantic perspective, yet the narrative provides realistic details of the city's terrain and the tavern on the dock opposite 5 South Street. "In the spring of 1840, the attention of the New York police was attracted by the many cases of well-known men found drowned in the vicarious waters surrounding the lower portion of our great city. Among these may be mentioned the name of Elwood Henderson, the noted tea merchant, whose remains were washed ashore at Redhook Point..." (237). Facts of the crimes linked to the river and the procedures of the Metropolitan Police are credible. History supports Green's narrative. According to J. D. McCabe, the river thieves were an especially fearsome criminal class. He identifies " 'Slaughter House Point,' the intersection of James and South Streets, and so called by the police because of the many murders which have occurred there,... [as] the principal rendevous of the East River thieves" (535). The memoirs of Police Chief George Walling also describes the menace of the river thieves under the leadership of the notorious Mike Shannon (534).

Against this realistic background, Green employs one of her unique mechanical devices at the crux of the mystery. The mathematical presentation of the device used by the criminals assures the reader that the disappearances occurred by "natural," if devious means. A pair of doors—one opening on a staircase and the second opening on a chute leading to the river below—are designed to confuse and then dispose of unwary victims who meet their deaths by drowning. Green heightens the mystery by focusing on the isolation of the tavern: "The night was dark and the river especially so,...and saving the gruff singing of some drunken sailor coming from a narrow side street near by, no sound disturbed the somewhat lugubrious silence of this weird and forsaken spot" (242).

Green avoids the tendency to overload "Staircase at Heart's Delight" with romantic twists and peripheral situations. Instead, there is a balance between realism and romanticism. The structure of the short narrative works well—Green avoids a moralistic ending by having the ever-practical Ebenezer Gryce comment on the fact that he was lucky to survive that venture: "The mystery was solved, and my footing on the force secured; but to this day—and I am an old man now—I have not forgotten the horror of the moment when my feet slipped from under me, and I felt myself sliding downward, without hope of rescue, into a pit of heaving waters, where so many men of conspicuous virtue had already ended their valuable lives" (259).

When a detective has the task of solving a puzzle, the narrative may tend to be simplistic or, to the other extreme, so complicated that the reader is either bored or burdened. Green's stories work best when there is a balance. And when she leavens the story with humor—one of the distinctive qualities that Gryce possesses—the lively characterization keeps the story from dragging, alleviating the heavy tone that burdens some of her other stories. Green's most successful stories have characteristic features: a setting evoking mystery, a clever puzzle, a surprise ending, and an interplay of motifs. Those stories which offer a slice of American life are fresher and more authentic.

Fiction became Green's most effective medium. Had she lived in 1988 instead of 1888, she might have found a more open market for her poetry and drama. The fact remains that despite all odds, she was determined to find a place for herself as a professional writer. She made choices based on the response of the American publishing establishment, and she succeeded. She wrote novels, novelets, and short stories; she developed qualities which were to distinguish her fiction. And, as we shall see in subsequent chapters, Green not only wrote good mystery fiction, but she also captured significant aspects of nineteenth century American life.

Chapter 4
Conventions and Influence

In the second half of the nineteenth century when Green was searching for recognition as a writer, detective fiction was developing into a distinct genre. It appealed to the newly industrialized nations in Europe and the United States—societies seeking practical solutions to social problems. As literature in which man's rationality prevails, detective fiction offers a medium for re-structuring the environment through the powers of a detective. Although frequently drawn from real-life situations, the literary representation of the detection process transforms reality. Consequently, the aesthetic structure of detective fiction, including its many conventions, was shaped by the pioneers in the genre.

When Green adopted the detective story, she used conventions developed by Poe, Gaboriau, and Collins, but she was not an imitator. She transformed the detective story from a European to an American model. Her fiction has distinct characteristics, each transformed by her own experience; these include setting, puzzle structure, motifs, prose style, and serial detectives. (Because of the range of her serial detectives and the number of works in which they appear, I have reserved analysis of her detectives for Chapter Five.)

Unlike Poe, Green did not look to Europe as the setting for her fiction. Instead she chose to write about the environment she knew best—New York, Manhattan, and the villages of the Hudson Valley.[1] *One of My Sons* (1901), for example, begins as the door of a Fifth Avenue brownstone opens and a young girl rushes out into the street to ask for help. Archibald Gillespie, stockbroker and railroad merchant, owns the house which is also inhabited by his three sons, their wives, and a grandchild. This is a house that proclaims the social status of its owner: "The hall, was seen from the entrance, was wide and unusually rich. Indeed, an air of the highest respectability, as well as of unbounded wealth, characterized the whole establishment..." (2). This was also the kind of house readers clamored to enter, fueled by the society pages of New York's dailies.

But in the same novel, we also see another side of New York, lower Manhattan, a ghetto area where the poor live. A daughter-in-law of Archibald Gillespie who has run away from home and family is found living miserably in a lower Manhattan tenement. Even though Green did not personally experience poverty, she knew it well by reputation and from the daily tabloids. Nevins indicates that "readers of newspapers could turn from an account of some sumptuous banquet at Delmonico's restaurant in New York...to a record of the police charging half-starved working-men, or a description of want and disease in the congested tenements" (201). As one historian points out, "...the slums...by 1900 housed more than one and a half million of the city's residents. Many European observers, especially visitors of the eighties, contended that these quarters exceeded in misery the worst that London and Paris could offer; and American writers like Jacob Riis and William Dean Howells presented even more graphic evidence of the squalor in which increasing thousands of New Yorkers dwelt" (Still 211). Green plays on the very real contrast between the lifestyles of the privileged and the deprived to create mystery, rendering both settings realistically. She describes in *One of My Sons* how Leighton Gillespie, an heir to his father's fortune, lives a lonely, unfulfilled life on Fifth Avenue, cow-towing to his father's demands; and also how Milles Fleurs, Leighton's wife, becomes prey to drugs and disease in a downtown hovel. In a sense, Green put New York on the literary map, making it equal to London or Paris as a center for mystery and intrigue.

However, Green was also well acquainted with village life and located many stories in rural areas. The town which is the setting for *Hand and Ring* (1883) is typical—Sibley is a small town situated upstate New York. Details of life in the community become important when the widow Clemmens is murdered, seemingly under the very eyes of its citizens. Green examines land entitlements, hidden relationships, routines of business and social life, railroad schedules and travel opportunities. Although far from the clamor and crime of Manhattan, this distant town has its secrets. In some novels, like *Lost Man's Lane* (1898), Green does not identify the village by name, thus creating an illusion of mystery: "Some ninety miles from here in a more or less inaccessible region, there is a small but interesting village, which has been the scene of so many unaccountable disappearances that the attention of the New York police has at last been directed to it. . . .[It] is one of those quiet, placid little spots found now and then among the mountains. . ." (5). Although Green develops the small town as effectively as the city, the glamour which "Gotham" conjured up in the imagination of the public made the city a more appealing setting to most readers— a factor which may have influenced Green to choose it for most of her stories.

At the heart of every detective story is a puzzle whose design is as unique as the author's signature. According to Cawelti, "writers who chose to develop longer and more complex stories had to find a number of ways of resolving the inevitable tension between the detection-mystification structure with the detective at the center and the variety of other interests. . ." (110). The detection-mystification structure which became Green's trademark is based on sets of doubles. The doubles motif involves sets of like characters (two sisters, two brothers, or two families); settings (two homes, two localities); crimes (double murders or two related crimes); detectives (the professional and the amateur sleuth). Disguise and impersonation provide additional sets. Solving the puzzle is thus complicated by the variety of possible combinations. Although some combinations, like the dark lady and the albino in *Behind Closed*

Doors (1888), seem stretched beyond belief, others are highly effective. In *The Woman in the Alcove* (1906), for example, Green manipulates two disparate settings—Manhattan and a mining town in New Mexico, two suitors, two detectives, and two murders. In *A Matter of Millions* (1890), Green multiplies the number of contenders who qualify as the heiress known as Jenny Rogers. Among several possibilities are Virginia Rogers, Jenny Rogers, and Jeannette Rogers, and each of them comes from radically different backgrounds. Along with the women are sets of suitors and families, each playing a hidden role in the mystery. As in typical Green puzzles, in these novels the links between the sets are forged by a series of clues; solving the puzzle is achieved when all of the components fit together.

Green employed motifs used by her predecessors, but she gave two motifs—the house and the unusual mechanical device—new life. Though the old or haunted house has traditionally been a gothic motif (Radcliffe xii), Green uses houses in a variety of *other* ways. There are no castles—just stalwart American structures. Some houses are simply functional dwellings, nothing more; others reveal wealth or social class (like the cottage in "Midnight in Beauchamp Row"); while others are true gothic places, with secret spaces, houses where tragedies have occurred (like the Heart's Delight Tavern). Because Green defines environment as significant to behavior, it is appropriate that she focuses on the house. We see this in virtually every plot. Typically, a house like the Leavenworth residence (in Green's first novel) is designated not by its address, but rather by the family name—thus the "Leavenworth house." In single-focus short stories like "The House in the Mist," "The Forsaken Inn," and "The Old Stone House," each of the dwellings is central to the mystery and has its own tragedy to reveal. The old stone house, for example, stands unfinished and abandoned. In reading an antiquated diary, a visitor discovers that the house was to be the home of Colonel Schuyler and young Juliet who died suddenly under mysterious circumstances in the house. How did she die?

The evidence remains in the decaying house, as the reader subsequently discovers.

Almost every house in Green's fiction contains a secret panel, closet, or passageway: *A Step on the Stair* features a house with a hidden staircase; *The Mayor's Wife* contains a secret passageway between two old houses; *The Millionaire Baby* has a summer house with a subterranean chamber.

The Filigree Ball takes place at the "Moore house" in Washington, D.C. which "antedates the Capitol and the White House" (6). We learn that although "it bears to this day the impress of large ideas and quiet elegance,...families that have moved in have as quickly moved out, giving as their excuse that no happiness was to be found there and that sleep was impossible under its roof" (6). The reader is invited by the narrator to uncover the secret hidden in the house and, in a sense, to exorcise its ghosts.

Green also developed stories around mechanical devices. She had a genuine interest in science, a kind of Yankee ingenuity, and recognized that the public shared that interest. Living in Buffalo, a city that was pioneering in the harnessing of electricity, Green witnessed the development of industry. And the work of her husband, Charles Rohlfs, made her even more intimately aware of the possibilities of invention. Rohlfs was a mechanical engineer who delighted in new designs; for instance, he invented one of the first chafing dishes and built clocks with unusual timing devices.[2] Anna shared her husband's interests, often testing out inventions of her own in fiction. We see this in such devices as the electrical system in *The Circular Study,* the airplane in *Initials Only,* the signalling device in "The Bronze Hand," and the poisoned coils in "The Little Steel Coils." But the deadly settle in *The Filigree Ball,* was perhaps her most controversial of devices. This involved a weight attached to a hidden pulley situated over the hearthstone in the parlor of the Moore house. The weight, when lowered on an unsuspecting victim, would case a fatal concussion—yet no wound would be obvious. Carolyn Wells found fault with the device, denouncing it as "an unsure mode of death" (468). But the criticism is perhaps unfair, for Green describes the device in painstaking detail complete with illustrations. In this case as in others, Green makes the unusual credible. She plays on the public's fear of the unknown, the haunted house, and the strange occurrence, but she turns this fear around, providing a logical explanation. Thus the mechanical device is part of the mystery puzzle, not a deus ex machina.

As the link between Poe and his American descendants, Anna Katharine Green holds a significant position in the field of detective fiction. We can trace her influence in the works of scores of writers who adopted the conventions and in the motifs that she helped to develop. Green became especially important to other female authors in the United States and Europe who perceived her as a pioneer and mentor. In her analysis of American detective fiction, Joan Mooney perceives Carolyn Wells and Mary Roberts Rinehart as Green's immediate successors (99). Following Wells and Rinehart is one of the most famous women writers influenced by Green— Agatha Christie.

Agatha Christie had been introduced to Green's fiction as an adolescent and recounts being especially taken with the two heroines in *The Leavenworth Case (An Autobiography* 147). Over forty years had passed since the first printing of *The Leavenworth Case* when Christie published her first novel *The Mysterious Affair at Styles* in 1920. Yet, in comparing the fiction of the two authors, the reader may readily see parallels between Green's work and Christie's— in the aging male detectives, Gryce and Poirot; in the wise spinsters, Amelia Butterworth and Jane Marple, in the young amateur sleuths who assist the police. Both Green and Christie also construct mathematical puzzles, using sets of components to complicate the puzzle. (Christie was to expand the sets into larger and more flexible groups as in *Ten Little Indians* and *Murder on the Orient Express*.) And like Green, Christie focuses on the house, the country estate or the city townhouse, as the center of conflict, revealing the secrets of the home and its occupants.

Mary Roberts Rinehart, however, is the most direct descendant of Green in the female line of American detective fiction writers and, as such, offers perhaps the most telling study in comparison. Like Christie, she also acknowledged Green's influence, recounting how she picked out a novel by Green from her bookshelf, noted the publisher, Bobbs Merrill, and sent out her manuscript of *The Circular Staircase* to that publisher *(My Story* 446). In 1914 Rinehart produced a detective duo similar to Green's Ebenezer Gryce and Amelia Butterworth—George Patton and Hilda Adams (also known as Miss Pinkerton). Patton, like Gryce, is a professional detective; Hilda Adams, however, is different from Butterworth—a more modern heroine, she is a trained nurse, a young woman who is self-supporting. As a nurse, she is admitted as a trusted employee into the homes of wealthy, but troubled people. Rinehart also uses doubles, like Green, to layer the levels of complexity, and she also focuses on the house and the family structure.

Yet there is a stylistic difference between Green and Rinehart. The difference is significant to understanding why contemporary readers are more likely to have read Rinehart, or at least to know of her, while Green remains relatively unknown except to students of the genre. Green's style is the key factor. During her lifetime, critics were generally supportive of Green's work. There were exceptions, of course, but she was generally well respected. *NYT* critics, for example, tended to give her good reviews, such as the following for *The House of the Whispering Pines* (1910):

Anna Katharine Green is a master hand at the weaving of spider-web plots of mystification, the piling up of small bits of evidence that will seem to implicate the innocent, but finally will be made to fit, plain and damning, into the scheme whereby the guilty one is brought to justice (*NYT*, 15, 26 March 1910, 163).

But a review of *Dark Hollow* (1914) focused on elements of style that were to be viewed by subsequent generations of readers as limitations:

The portentous seriousness of speech, the long sentences and the formal phrases that the novelist puts into the mouths of her characters make its scenes anything but real. And of course there should be some illusion of reality even in a detective story *(Boston Transcript,* 14 February 1914, 6).

The "diffuse" quality of Green's prose can be explained both by her age (she was fifty years older than Rinehart) and by her preference for formal rhetoric. But by the turn of the century, prose style was becoming more colloquial. We can see the features of Green's style by contrasting a segment of her prose with that of Mary Roberts Rinehart. I have selected two comparable works for examination, both published during the same period, 1914-1915. Green's *The Golden Slipper* and Rinehart's "The Buckled Bag" feature young women, amateur sleuths who solve puzzles threatening a socially prominent family. Green's heroine, Violet Strange, is a New York debutante, while Rinehart's Hilda Adams is a nurse who comes from Chicago's middle class. Each woman is aggressive, determined, and smart. Yet the most striking differences between the two characters have less to do with social class than with the authors' styles.

Consider the following excerpts from the stories:
From Green's *The Golden Slipper:*
The third person narrator describes Violet Strange:

She was a small, slight woman whose naturally quaint appearance was accentuated by the extreme simplicity of her attire...no other personality could vie with hers in strangeness, or in the illusive quality of her ever-changing expression. She was vivacity incarnate and, to the ordinary observer, light as thistledown in fibre and in feeling. But not to all. To those who watched her long, there came moments— say when the music rose to heights of greatness—when the mouth so given over to laughter took on curves of the rarest sensibility, and a woman's lofty soul shone through her odd, bewildering features.

    Driscoll had noted this...(5)

From Rinehart's: "The Buckled Bag":
Miss Adams is the first person narrator; she recounts Detective Patton's observations of her own character:

"You have a good head, Miss Adams," he said to me one day when he was almost well. "Are you going to spend the rest of your life changing pillowslips and shaking down a thermometer?... You've stood a cracking test and come through A one. You've got silence and obedience to orders, and you have a brain." (9).

The descriptions of the two women are marked by differences in voice, in language, and in focus. Green employs a third person narrator, whereas Rinehart gives the authority of the narrator to Hilda Adams. The speaker in the Violet Strange stories is the author-narrator; Violet is *not* empowered to speak for herself. In contrast, Hilda Adams is in a position of power as narrator. She recounts directly what George Patton has said to her, in his own terms—clearly the words of a policeman looking for a stealthy assistant. According to Robert Champigny, "Mystery stories alert the reader to the importance of the fictional viewpoint" (68). The "outside" narrator places distance between Violet Strange and the reader—this gap tends to disengage the reader from the detection process. With Hilda Adams, the reader is at her elbow, going through the paces of the detective along with her.

Even though they were both writing during the same time period, Green is wordy and illusive, while Rinehart is stark and direct. "Small, slight" and "odd, bewildering," are examples of the double adjectives Green often used—a practice that tends to slow the pace of her sentences. Consider also the ambiguity in Green's phrases: "no other personality could vie with hers in its strangeness, or in the elusive quality of her ever changing expression;" and "a woman's lofty soul shone through her odd, bewildering features." In contrast, Rinehart uses adjectives sparingly and makes no poetic allusions: "You've got a good head, Miss Adams." Green's syntax is further complicated by lengthy passages spoken by the outside narrator. Rinehart's story relies almost entirely on dialogue, which keeps the pace lively.

The prose of these stories affects characterization as well as reader appeal. Green's portrait of Violet Strange is romantic. The "adorned" prose focuses on the heroine's beauty and femininity, which dominates even though her actions testify to her intelligence and strength. I suggest that this conception of the heroine is a carry-over from the tradition of the myth of the "fair maiden," which critics of nineteenth century fiction have identified.[3] Rinehart, on the other hand, underplays Hilda's beauty and femininity. Although Patton later admits to Hilda: "There's only one objection—you're too good looking" (9), he is struck first by her intellectual ability and moral toughness. Hilda Adams, when she surveys herself in the mirror and sees the "lines" that say, "Twenty-nine, almost thirty" (10), rejects being labelled "good-looking." Since Rinehart's treatment is realistic, the lack of adornment in the author's prose is appropriate. And this may well be the nub of the issue—that Green's language did not change with time, that even though she was still publishing in the 1920s, her fiction is written in the linguistic style of the nineteenth century.

Yet in 1878, Green was using the vernacular of the day, and writing her stories from real life situations. Her novels and short fiction reflect the concerns of her own generation—a people who had celebrated their centennial, who were enjoying the luxuries of a newly industrialized society. She portrays the American experience in her work, often focusing on the problems of the vulnerable, the likely victims. Her detective fiction offers insight into the unique culture of nineteenth century America, displaying not only the glamour of Fifth Avenue, but also the commonplace realities of ordinary Americans.

Chapter Five
Detectives

The detective is a special person—according to detective fiction enthusiasts. Readers look for an individual who commands respect, who can solve mind-boggling puzzles. Readers also expect to develop a rapport with the detective, especially with a serial detective who becomes more familiar with each succeeding adventure. For the author and publisher, the lure of the detective's persona assures future sales as readers look forward to renewing their acquaintance with a trusted figure.

Anna Katharine Green not only understood the role of the detective, but she also had a talent for perceiving the kind of persona readers would find appealing. Realizing that the public enjoyed keeping in touch with fictional heroes and heroines, Green developed five serial detectives—three men and two women. The most famous is Inspector Ebenezer Gryce of the New York Metropolitan Police Force. An older man who ages along with his clients, Gryce is often assisted by two young police recruits—Detectives Horace Byrd and Caleb Sweetwater. Sweetwater, however, appears in more stories than Byrd and matures with Gryce to develop his own reputation.

Green's two female sleuths, Amelia Butterworth and Violet Strange, are members of New York's elite society. Amelia Butterworth is a spunky matron who assists Ebenezer Gryce in cases where her feminine insights and social access are needed. Emerging at the turn of the century is Violet Strange, a new breed of woman—young and rebellious, independent and enterprising. She does not

assist Gryce or any other policeman, nor does she "play" at detection
to allay boredom. A private detective, she is paid for her services.

Unlike her predecessors or successors in the genre, Green created
a network of detectives whose lives connect within the New York
environment. Although she developed individual mysteries which
took place in areas outside the metropolitan area (New England,
Chicago, Washington D.C., New Mexico, for example), her serial
detectives operate in the New York area. Except for Violet Strange,
they are friends and family to Ebenezer Gryce, the patriarch among
her detectives, who provided stability and recognition to their
fictional exploits. To solve puzzles, they each use induction and,
as Regis Messac points out, an incredible amount of "patience"
(577).

Ebenezer Gryce

When Ebenezer Gryce first puts in an appearance in *The
Leavenworth Case* in 1878, he is already an older man—settled in
his ways and established in his profession. Gryce does not change
remarkably in the forty-five years between his first appearance and
his last in *The Hasty Arrow* (1917), nor does he age significantly.
The "portly, comfortable personage with an eye that never pounced,
that did not even rest—on you" (*LC* 7) became an international
celebrity because he was a well-conceived character. An American
policeman with middle-class values, Gryce is the man-next-door,
a kindly individual who inspires trust. Building on initial reader
response to Gryce, Green sustained interest in his exploits by adding
dimensions to his character in succeeding works and by including
cohorts who were to become like members of his family.

Gryce is likely to have been drawn from living models—fleshed
out with the qualities of two men whom Green admired—the Chief
of the New York Metropolitan Police Force and her father. Certainly,
Gryce's reality as a character accounts for his success. Green
recounted how she often accompanied her father and the Chief of
Police on carriage rides to Long Island ("Why Human Beings Are
Interested in Crime" 84). She refrained from mentioning the man

by name, but given the time, the Police Chief is likely to have been John Jourdan or James Kelso, either may well have been a source for Gryce.[1] It is also likely that qualities of her own father were realized in Gryce, for James Wilson Green was an acknowledged model. In *The Sword of Damocles* (1881), Green's dedication reveals his influence: "To my Father, I dedicate this book as expressing some of the principles of Justice and Mercy, by Precept and Example, he has instilled into my breast from early childhood." Gryce emerges as distinctly American, middle-class, and practical in his approach to solving problems. Although knowledgeable of the law and its application, he is distinguished by his humanistic values and his unpretentious bearing.

In fact, Gryce's foibles are his most memorable features. His habit of not looking directly at the person he is interrogating, his wry smiles, and his rheumatoid arthritis make him human. The incongruity of the great detective unable to face his suspects has its humor (and Green uses this ploy to advantage.) Thus when Inspector Gryce scrutinizes Mary Leavenworth *(The Leavenworth Case)*, we are told that "his eye never left the coffee urn upon which it had fixed itself at her first approach" (108). The apparent shyness so characteristic of Gryce may be a ploy to catch the unwary off-guard, but it may also reflect some insecurity in social situations. A gentleman neither by birth nor education, Ebenezer Gryce is a self-made man. His one admitted limitation is that he cannot pass himself off as a gentleman, despite the fact that he is adept at disguise. He once confided to his young assistant, "I have even employed a French valet, who understands dancing and whiskers, but it was all of no avail" (*LC* 149). But this is part of Gryce's charm and probably accounts for his popularity among middle-class readers.

Yet Gryce is not average; his inner strength and integrity, his stalwart pursuit of truth and justice distinguish him. The narrator of *The Leavenworth Case* directs the reader to consider the depth of Gryce's character: "...when I stood before (Gryce's) neat three story brick house...I could not but acknowledge there was something in the aspect of its half-open shutters over closely drawn curtains of spotless purity, highly suggestive of the character of its inmate" (144). The less obvious qualities are suggested not only by Gryce's home, but also by his bearing and values. Though not identified with a particular church, his orientation is distinctly Calvinistic. After solving a crime, Gryce's method involves a kind of regenerative rite—as we have seen in his treatment of Mary Leavenworth, where she is given the chance to repudiate past mistakes and re-establish her integrity. Thus, entrapment is not the end of his detectival efforts, but rather the restoration of decency and order.

When he relates to people, Gryce is not judgmental, however. He is non-committal and usually self-effacing. Green presents him with feet of clay—and with bandages, no less, when his rheumatism flares up. Always the practical man, Gryce hires people to do his leg-work when time and effort are at stake. Often the person is young and physically adept. Gryce's cohorts not only assist in the pursuit of criminals, but they also add an interesting dimension to the old detective's character. According to tradition, Mr. Gryce is a loner—a sleuth unfettered by family connections and dedicated to his profession. The reader learns that he is a widower with a beloved grandchild living in South America. However, he does have friends: with Amelia Butterworth he develops a quasi-romantic relationship; in Caleb Sweetwater, his young protege in the Metropolitan Police Force, he discovers the son he never had.

In Ebenezer Gryce, Green produced a detective who appealed to her nineteenth century audience—a person to whom they could relate. The serial detective has to be the kind of character that readers want to encounter again. Gryce's appeal lies in his non-threatening facade, his ordinary humanity reinforced by qualities people of his generation admired: common sense, dedication to work, and solid moral values. While *The Leavenworth Case* established his reputation, *A Strange Disappearance* (1880) confirmed his status as a serial detective. In her second novel Green focuses on the fact that this is Gryce's second appearance by having the narrator comment on his success in *The Leavenworth Case*. (This method of internal sequencing of adventures has since become an accepted technique among writers of serial detective stories.) The narrator compares the disappearance of the young heroine, Luttra, with that of Hannah in Gryce's first case. Then the concerned housekeeper who reports the lady missing asks directly for Detective Gryce because she has heard about him and wants expert assistance. Although he does less physical work this time, Gryce is the brains behind the scene. Early on, he has to deal with Holman Blake, an arrogant upper-class type who might easily threaten the average policeman. But Gryce meets him directly and establishes his own authority. In directing the activities of his leg-men, Gryce reasons that the criminals who are holding the woman hostage are hiding nearby; he also develops a rescue plan and is on hand when the group is taken by surprise and arrested. The novel does not end simply with the release of the heroine, however. Once again, Gryce plays judge and priest, warning the culprits: "Old scores shall be raked up against you" (250), implying that if they do not keep silent about the victim's past, he will pursue all the former charges against them and make their prison terms much longer. By silencing their threats, he saves the woman's reputation and protects her marriage.

Yet Gryce does not always keep the upper-hand as we see in *A Matter of Millions* (1891). In this novel, he makes two big mistakes: he arrests the wrong man and is duped by a con-woman (a rarity in the Green canon). Perhaps Green was setting the scene for Gryce's retirement, for she casts him as "an old man now, verging on to seventy, and both from age and infirmity in no condition to engage in the active exercise of...detective work" (79-80). To offset his encroaching age, Green introduces Mr. Horace Byrd as an alter ego. An attractive and cultivated young man, Byrd has a distinct advantage in dealing with crime in high society. Plodding along in his low-key fashion, Gryce appears tired and lack-lustre next to Byrd—he even brings murder charges against the innocent Hamilton De Graw. However, Gryce ultimately fits the pieces of the puzzle together correctly. By determining that a charwoman would not have bought expensive bonbons for herself, that only an adventuress would allow herself to be seen at night unescorted, that a schoolgirl is withholding information—Gryce identifies the murderer.

Despite the acclaim Gryce earns for his efforts, he is thoroughly embarrassed at being duped by a con-woman who escapes through a secret exit in a closet while he sits in her chamber waiting to arrest her. Yet Gryce's chagrin only adds to the reader's delight. The reader can sympathize and laugh with the unwary detective; the touch lightens the novel and rejuvenates Gryce. Green also uses down-to-earth scenes, such as the one between Gryce and the schoolgirl, Jenny Rogers, to emphasize Gryce's rapport. With this obstinate youngster, Gryce projects a fatherly image as he coaxes the truth from her about a clandestine meeting. "You look so good," she says and then proceeds to confide in him (96). Gryce's talent for inviting disclosure on the part of suspects gives him the edge in solving the mystery. Green effectively filters the details of crime with humor, thus increasing Gryce's humanity and adding to the reader's entertainment. Humor also neutralizes the effects of melodrama and moralism—two elements which tend to burden Green's style.

As if deciding to resuscitate Ebenezer Gryce, Green injects new life into her hero in the short story, "Staircase at Heart's Delight" (1894). A flashback on Gryce's start with the Metropolitan Police Force, the story recounts how he emerges as a young man anxious to make a name for himself. By impersonating a potential victim, Gryce is lured to the lower West Side of Manhattan, to a tavern on the docks. Bodies of wealthy New Yorkers have been found in the Hudson River, the apparent victims of drowning. A willing but cautious Gryce allows himself to be led to an upper room in the tavern where he discovers the mystery of the infamous staircase. After surviving a dunk in the chilly waters of the West Side, the illustrious career of Ebenezer Gryce gets its start. "Staircase at Heart's Delight" is a classic in its own right—a romantic tale of old New York which continues to entertain mystery lovers. As part of Gryce's personal history the story is also significant: it not only reaffirms the author's decision to keep him active but it also creates an aura of romance, giving the old detective a legendary past.

When Gryce puts in his next appearance in *Hand and Ring* (1883) disguised as a red-haired hunchback, his skill at impersonation has become an art. The cover is so effective, in fact, that not even the reader discovers that Gryce was at the scene until much later in the course of the investigation. In this case, Mr. Horace Byrd is again working as a police investigator, and though he has neither the experience nor the reputation of Mr. Gryce, he does most of the heavy work. As a young man "by birth and education a gentleman," he has entree to the social circles of the primary suspects. Gryce emerges well into the case as a consultant to Byrd, but the younger man clearly overshadows the elusive Gryce in both visibility and charm. Perhaps Green was trying out Byrd as a possible replacement for Gryce and, apparently, she decided in Gryce's favor. Mr. Byrd makes a solo appearance to solve the mystery of Mrs. Manchester's missing necklace ("Three Thousand Dollars"), but then he disappears from Green's fictional world.

Amelia Butterworth

A more successful relationship develops between Gryce and Amelia Butterworth who offers her services as an amateur sleuth. While Horace Byrd and Ebenezer Gryce are professional colleagues, Miss Butterworth becomes more than merely an assistant—she and Gryce share a friendship which has an aura of courtship. An older, unmarried woman, Amelia Butterworth enjoys considerable social status. "A woman of inborn principle and strict Presbyterian training," Miss Butterworth holds court in her Gramercy Park brownstone (*Lost Man's Lane* v). Green recounted that she knew a woman of "the best society in one of our large cities" who helped the police ("Why Human Beings Are Interested In Crime" 39). The reality of such a person may account for the facile characterization of this society matron who was to achieve recognition as one of Green's most memorable characters. But it is even more likely that Green built upon the role played by the real woman by giving

Miss Butterworth qualities of an elderly woman she knew intimately. A likely model for Amelia Butterworth was Sarah Elizabeth Green, the author's "mother-sister." The elder Miss Green was indeed "a woman of in-born principle and strict Presbyterian training," as her cautionary letters to her younger sister reveal.[2] Butterworth's forte is her great skill in dealing with other women of all ages and backgrounds. Though Gryce's "fatherly" approach is successful with some women, he is ill at ease with many of the females he encounters.

When Butterworth meets Gryce for the first time in *That Affair Next Door* (1888), she notices his "portly and easy-going" appearance, his "spectacles," and his "half-admiring, half-sarcastic" tone of voice (14). What strikes her most strongly is his age, remarking that he looked "75 if he was a day" (14). (Her impressions also inform the reader of Gryce's condition.) However, she is not deterred by any of Gryce's peculiarities—if anything, she finds him a challenge; perhaps his age gives her a false sense of superiority. In her enthusiasm for the detective game, Butterworth has to prove herself to a reluctant Gryce in order to establish her credibility. The methods of Gryce and Butterworth are not that different: both are logical thinkers who use deductive as well as inductive reasoning. While Butterworth jots down her ideas on the back of a grocery list, Gryce keeps a notebook. And they both experience flashes of intuition. The basic difference between them is in their social conditioning. Gryce has been exposed to a variety of people in his work on the police force but is ill-at-ease with the wealthy and with most women. Butterworth's specialties are the upper class and women of all ages and classes.

When Louise Van Burnam is found murdered in the brownstone next door, Amelia Butterworth offers her assistance to the police. The puzzle is complicated by sets of doubles (a typical Green structure)—two Van Burnam sisters, two brothers and two wives. The first break in the case occurs when Miss Butterworth finds part of a hatpin (which Gryce quickly determines is the murder weapon), and then adroitly indicates to Gryce where the missing part of the pin might logically be found. As the investigation progresses, Butterworth proves her mettle in dealing with women. She locates a second woman seen at the house prior to the murder and then insinuates herself into the home of a young socialite who has hired the woman. She chats up the charwoman whom she feels has been withholding information and who then confirms her suspicions. She takes a midnight walk with her young housemaid to track down a missing bundle. (The two women make an amusing couple as they trudge at midnight unescorted into a Chinese laundry and derive useful information from the astonished proprietor.) She continues to apply feminine insight into matching up suspects with the clothes they wear, thus determining social class and refinements of taste not apparent to an "outsider." Some women buy their hats on Fifth Avenue, but others insist on Parisian imports; Altman's or Arnold's are the "in" places for purchasing good quality fabric. Butterworth applies years of experience to the psychology of clothes and comes up with information which Gryce would be hard-pressed to get on his own.

While Butterworth makes her conquests, Gryce takes on the men. In fact, he is at the point of arresting one of the Van Burnam brothers. All efforts come to a screeching halt, however, after Butterworth and Gryce compare notes. Gryce is so humbled by her apparent success that he considers resigning from the Force. Ironically, neither one of them has been correct in deducing the identity of the murderer. And it is only when Butterworth and Gryce put their heads together that they are able to put clues into perspective and make accurate deductions.

Gryce acknowledges Butterworth's talent and thanks her for her help. He sees the value in "women's eyes for women's matters" (59). And Butterworth respects Gryce's skill, but she is not self-effacing: "I am as sly as he, and though not quite as old—now I am sarcastic—have some of his wits, if but little of his experience" (57). Amelia Butterworth's self-image is extremely positive, so positive that she is comfortable mocking herself. For example, when the Van Burnam daughters treat her with less deference than she

deems appropriate, Miss Butterworth retaliates. She puts out her
best china in entertaining the young ladies, but deletes an entree
from the menu so that the meal is sparse: "Was I going to allow
these proud young misses to think I had exerted myself to please
them?" (44). Although Butterworth does not tolerate the snubs of
the elite, she is sensitive to women in distress and, as the case reveals,
she protects and offers sanctuary to one such woman—Olive
Randolph, the wife abandoned by the murderer. As we shall see
in Chapter Seven, Amelia Butterworth raises the consciousness of
the public to the plight of women who have minimal legal protection
in marriage.

As a detective duo, Gryce and Butterworth compliment each
other. He is manly, a representative of the middle-class, a self-made
man; she is feminine, upper-class, and highly moral. Their values
provide common ground for working together, and their lively
camaraderie surpasses merely the rivalry of two sleuths. As
Butterworth admits in *Lost Man's Lane* (1898), she realizes that
Gryce maneuvers her into assisting him, that he is not merely
interested in light conversation: "I ought to have been on my guard.
I ought to have known the old fox well enough to feel certain
that when he went so out of his way to take me into his confidence
he did it for a purpose: (3). When Gryce gives her the details of
the Knollys' case, he is making a bid for her services. And
Butterworth, though she plays hard to get, enjoys the cajoling and
welcomes the opportunity to help. Aside from the diversion that
such activity would bring, she has an even greater motive for
volunteering her services, believing that it is an "opportunity...for
a direct exercise of my detective powers in a line seemingly laid
out for me by Providence...." (3). The Gryce-Butterworth alliance
is thus a serious moral commitment, not just a game.

When Miss Butterworth learns that an old friend's home has
become the locus of a series of mysterious disappearances, she accepts
the challenge from Mr. Gryce to investigate. Unknown to both them
at the start, this case will place Amelia Butterworth in mortal danger,
in a direct encounter with a psychopathic murderer. Althea Knollys

has died, but her children still occupy the family home in upstate New York. The house is located on Lost Man's Lane, so named for the disappearances. The house itself is so forbidding that Butterworth reports, "...never in my life had my eyes fallen upon a habitation more given over to neglect or less promising in hospitality" (33). The environment is realized in gothic detail as Butterworth encounters rattling doors, screams in the night, footsteps in unoccupied rooms, and a phantom coach. Although the Knollys children are reluctant to have her in the house and give her the least desirable bedroom, Butterworth firmly demands to stay.

Thus Miss Butterworth works alone in the desolate house, taking up residence in a bare, distant room with no lock on the door and no bell rope to summon aid. She comes equipped, however, with candles, an alcohol lamp, and appurtenances to brew tea. Not put off by the village types who regard her with suspicion, she extends herself to people and gradually wins over even the most recalcitrant individuals. By gathering information from the villagers, she is able to prevent another disappearance. More like a pioneer woman than a society matron, she takes risks in order to discover the truth. By insinuating herself into the confidence of the townsfolk, she becomes a threat to the murderer and a likely victim. Sensing danger lurking at her heels, Butterworth is plucky; yet, she has one crushing weakness—fear of dogs. One of the comic scenes in the novel portrays her cowering after an encounter with Saracen, the Knollys' dog. Nevertheless, it is not the dog who poses the real threat, but a man with a romantic interest in her—a man who was once in love with her friend, Althea Knollys.

Gryce's role is minimal in this novel. He maintains a contact in the town to ensure Miss Butterworth's safety, but she is the active agent in the case. Although Gryce appears on the scene in the nick of time to hold a pistol on the murderer, it is Butterworth who has penetrated the secret of Lost Man's Lane and risked her life in trapping the murderer. The double standard of Gryce dealing with the men and Butterworth with the women does not operate in this case, for Butterworth is on her own. Of the three Butterworth/ Gryce adventures, this is the one that establishes her reputation as an amateur sleuth. When she confides to Gryce that she received marriage proposals from two of the principals in the case—including the murderer, Gryce not only consoles her, but also intimates that he also finds her desirable: "I know many a worthy man who would like to follow their example" (385). Butterworth is touched by his response: "And with a low bow that left me speechless, Mr. Gryce laid his hand on his heart and softly withdrew" (385). Their relationship at this point seems to go beyond simply professional interest.

The Circular Study (1900) is the third and last case in which Amelia Butterworth assists Mr. Gryce. At the beginning, Gryce is told that this is a strange case—certainly, it reflects the turn of the century with electrical devices at the center of the mystery puzzle. Felix Adams, a mechanical genius, is found murdered in his New York City brownstone, his body locked behind the massive steel door in his circular study. Ebenezer Gryce is called to the scene, but responds somewhat reluctantly. We are told that Gryce has been "melancholy,... even contemplating resigning his position on the force and retiring to the little farm he had bought for himself in Westchester" (3). (Gryce's thoughts of retirement are similar to Hercule Poirot's attempt at growing vegetable marrow as a retirement project in *The Murder of Roger Ackroyd*.) But fortunately, Inspector Gryce finds Adams' murder sufficient challenge to continue his career, and Butterworth happily accepts Gryce's invitation to work with him.

Although Miss Butterworth tries not to appear pushy, she does not have to be coaxed into participating. She and Gryce are much more at ease with each other in this adventure. In fact, Butterworth has reached her stride; she is insightful, secure about her own abilities, and comfortable with Gryce. He seems glad of her enthusiasm and support. Together they return to the scene of the crime and observe the victim's valet as he reenacts what he remembers of the crime. The valet is both deaf and mute. Gryce discovers that the electrical signals in the room control a series of colored lights. Butterworth notices a worn spot in a corridor above the library; Gryce finds a peephole above it and deduces that the valet received orders from his master by means of the colored lights. Both he and Butterworth are convinced that the valet has been traumatized by the violence in the house, that he is not the guilty party.

Mr. Gryce coordinates all the detectival activities in the case. While he pulls together a series of seemingly unrelated clues in pursuit of the murderer, Caleb Sweetwater (who appeared in *A Strange Disappearance* (1880) plays a significant role in tracking down suspects. He discovers who the people were who visited Felix Adams on the day he was murdered by tracing the rose petals found at the scene of the crime. But the psychology of the crime is left to Mr. Gryce. He takes the young and recently married brother of the victim to Police Headquarters along with the man's father-in-law, supposedly for interrogation. Meanwhile Amelia Butterworth goes to work on the bride, Eva Poindexter Adams, believing that a woman will be better able to help. The mutual efforts of Butterworth and Gryce bring about the solution to the puzzle.

In this case, Ebenezer Gryce uses the ultimate discretion. Assuming the role of priest and judge, he allows the person who carried out the murder to go free, perceiving that the killing was a defensive act. The real culprit did not hold the knife in his hand, but as Amelia Butterworth proclaims, he is a "man without heart" (288). In agreeing that his crime was the greater before God and man, Butterworth and Gryce reveal their staunch Calvinistic values.

Gryce escorts Miss Butterworth home by carriage to her house in Gramercy Park. She vows that this will be her last case, while Gryce bows low and smiles, perhaps wondering if a case of similar interest will ever bring them together again.

Caleb Sweetwater
Up to this point, Sweetwater has been a stereotypical young

hirling whom Gryce sends out to accomplish energetic tasks. The more devious and cerebral adventures are undertaken by Gryce himself or by Amelia Butterworth. However, with the "retirement" of Miss Butterworth, the career of Caleb Sweetwater begins to ascend. Green appears to have planned for the development of Sweetwater, having cast him as the hero of *Agatha Webb* (1899). Gryce does not play a role in this novel; the unlikely home-town boy solves the mystery. *Agatha Webb* is not one of Green's most intriguing mysteries, but it does give the reader some insight into the character of Sweetwater. "...unattractive as he was in every way, ungainly in figure and unprepossessing of countenance, this butt of the more favoured youth in town had a heart whose secret fires were all the warmer for being so persistently covered..." (194): this description of young Sweetwater casts him as an anti-hero, the boy of good heart whose true worth is not appreciated by the community.

When the reader encounters Sweetwater in *Agatha Webb*, he is a local musician playing in an ensemble at the home of Mr. Sutherland, the town's leading citizen. His ungainly appearance and bright red hair distinguish Sweetwater, but it is not until a murder is discovered that his aspirations are revealed—we discover that he longs to become a detective. Sweetwater's motivation in the case is not completely self-serving, for he wishes to repay Mr. Sutherland a debt of kindness. Consequently, he strives to clear the name of the man's son in the murder of Agatha Webb. A veritable odyssey ensues with Sweetwater surviving a shipwreck, a den of thieves, and an unlikely hike along the New England coast. A cablegram from the Azores proves Sweetwater's hunch, that Norwegian sailors heard the cries of Agatha Webb's maid. And as the tale comes to an end, we are told that "Sweetwater was a made man" (359) from that day forward.

Presumably, Caleb Sweetwater leaves Sutherlandtown, in his native New England, and settles in New York City where he becomes a member of the Metropolitan Police Force. He leaves widowed mother behind as well as his violin. Among his new city friends is Ebenezer Gryce, who admires the unassuming young man's tenacity and enthusiasm. Literally, Sweetwater becomes the aging Gryce's arms and legs. While Gryce is the brains behind the scene, it is Sweetwater who hits the trail in hot pursuit. Green also develops an affective bond between the two men—something that was suggested, but never identified, in the Butterworth-Gryce relationship. The rules of propriety are not threatened by Sweetwater's filial devotion for Gryce—in fact, Gryce becomes a more human figure through the bonding. Actually, the relationship Sweetwater had with Mr. Sutherland in *Agatha Webb* foreshadows that with Gryce, portraying Sweetwater as a youth in need of a father-figure.

The thirty-two year old fiddler turned detective, once termed "more like an eel than a man" (116), makes his mark in New York City. He is on the scene after railway magnate Archibald Gillespie is murdered in his brownstone residence on Fifth Avenue *(One of My Sons* [1901]). Inspector Gryce conducts the investigation. Observers perceive Gryce as "a large, elderly man, with a world of experience in his time-worn but kindly visage" (56). Sweetwater initially seems muted, almost a shadowy figure next to Gryce; he is described only as "a young man...in attendance on the coroner" (59). Although Gryce, the "celebrated detective...had looks for nothing save the umbrella he rolled round and round between his palms" (138), his indirect manner is deceptive, for his observations are astute. And although his physical powers are diminished by age, he uses Sweetwater's vitality to advantage. At one point Gryce emerges from a taxi, assisted by Sweetwater, using crutches and hobbling about in the throes of a rheumatic attack.

Nevertheless, by combining mind and body, Gryce and Sweetwater solve this mystery. The major clue is identified by Gryce at the beginning of the investigation—a typed message found in the murdered man's typewriter. As each of the three heirs to their father's fortune become prime suspects, Gryce gathers and weighs evidence. The message appears to say, "one of my sons;" however, Sweetwater fortuitously discovers paste on the keys of the typewriter which obliterated the all important letter "N" before "one." The reinterpretation of the message clears the sons and places the guilt on the correct party. The Gryce-Sweetwater duo works effectively when each supports the other's activities. At no point does Sweetwater upstage his mentor, nor does Gryce pull rank with the young detective.

With *The Woman in the Alcove* (1906), Green may have been experimenting with a replacement for Ebenezer Gryce. Instead of Gryce, Inspector Dalzell coordinates the case with Sweetwater filling his usual role. This time, however, there is no evidence of a personal relationship between Sweetwater and the inspector. (Dalzell makes a single appearance in this novel.) Perhaps either the public or the author missed Gryce in this escapade, for Green phases out Dalzell and resuscitates Gryce in subsequent novels.

Sweetwater has become adept at coping with the unexpected. As we have seen in cases like *A Strange Disappearance* and *Agatha Webb*, he journeys to distant places when information is required and he infiltrates environments, often impersonating a local figure to gain insight into a situation. In *The Woman in the Alcove*, Sweetwater trails a suspect who is duped into hiring him as a valet. Not only does Sweetwater do what is expected of him, but he proves of invaluable assistance to his employer—scaling walls, tracking a missing contact, and maneuvering a row-boat in a highly suspicious rendevous. The agile Sweetwater catches an elusive man who has successfully evaded the law in both the East and Southwestern United States.

On their next caper together *Dark Hollow* (1911), both Gryce and Sweetwater have aged. But Sweetwater definitely gets top billing over the almost incapacited Gryce. At one point the sedentary old detective grumbles about traveling by subway and indulges himself by taking a taxi. In contrast, Sweetwater goes into action, displaying creativity as well as detectival acumen when socialite Edith Challoner is murdered right before the eyes of a startled public in a New York hotel.

Book II of the novel focuses almost exclusively on Sweetwater's activities as he investigates a similar crime which occurred years before in Brooklyn. The psychology of the crime strikes Sweetwater; he perceives a parallel between the murder of a washerwoman killed while standing at the window of her own room. In both cases the act is a feat of daring, almost in defiance of public scrutiny. We can see a change in the typical Gryce-Sweetwater pattern here, for now Sweetwater is doing the cerebral as well as the physical work, while Gryce remains in the background.

While observing his prey, Sweetwater assumes the identity of a carpenter. So careful is his cover that he actually labors in the trade. When he takes a room in the house where the suspect lives, he engages the man in friendship and then observes him (even to the point of constructing a peep hole between their rooms.) By fitting into this lower-class immigrant community, Sweetwater hopes to ferret out the truth about an individual whom he suspects is living under an assumed identity. Sweetwater places himself in some danger, but manages to discover how the suspect may be living a double life, and how he might be responsible for the death of Edith Challoner. Actually Book II of this novel is by far the best part, reflecting realistic and intriguing detection games. (Green goes off into a romantic, almost science-fiction, treatment in Book III which tends to make the novel uneven rather than sensational.)

Ebenezer Gryce is revived in *The Mystery of the Hasty Arrow* (1917)—his last case. Fortunately, he goes out in glory as he displays those qualities for which he has become celebrated. Though Sweetwater plays a significant role, he does not steal Gryce's fire. A rheumatic Inspector Gryce is called to a New York City museum to investigate the murder of a young French girl shot with a bow and arrow belonging to the museum collection. The case is difficult because witnesses are not truthful and hidden alliances must be unveiled if the puzzle is to be solved.

Gryce does some superb acting in order to elicit information from reluctant individuals. At one point he pretends to be completely debilitated in order to win the sympathy of a suspect's niece. She tells the poor old man all he needs to know to link her aunt with the victim. But in his efforts to locate the suspect, Gryce has to beguile a shopkeeper into revealing where the woman lives. He carries this off by pretending to be senile—his performance revealing that he is far from senile. By ordering fabric and asking the shopkeeper to send it to the woman, Gryce initiates an exciting sequence in which he has another detective trace the package and thus locate the suspect. Sweetwater does some of the legwork in tracking the elusive woman across Westchester to the Palisades and back to New York City. Ultimately though, the psychology of the crime and the mentality of the murderer are the essential elements in the puzzle. And here is where Gryce shines as an observer of humanity, a man who distinguishes between good and evil. The final moments in the story allow Gryce to observe a moment of truth and an affirmation of justice.

Violet Strange

With the publication of *The Golden Slipper* (1915), Green introduced a new female detective—Violet Strange. Unlike her counterpart, Amelia Butterworth, she is young and works at detection for pay. Concealing her activities from her wealthy father, Violet accepts cases from a private detective agency because she needs money. The question is, why? The reader is apprised that Violet has a hidden purpose for the money, but the truth is not revealed until her final adventure. With the creation of Violet Strange, Green developed a structure for nine separate short stories, all of which feature Miss Strange; the last story discloses her secret.

While Violet Strange could easily be kin to Amelia Butterworth in social class and ethical values, she is younger and far more liberated. At the publication of this collection, Anna Katharine Green was sixty years old. Her own daughter, Rosamund, was then Violet's age, so the author was well acquainted with the new generation of American women. This youthful heroine was an antidote to Green's increasing age. And the conception was a fresh one for Green who had written novels and unrelated short stories, but no collection with the structure of the Violet Strange stories. With her chestnut colored hair and small mobile face, Violet is like the flower; she is known as the "little detective." Her clientele comes mainly from the upper reaches of society, from people who trust her as one of their own. Although individuals have been known to claim supernatural powers for her, she is careful to counter that myth, pointing out that she "is nothing if not practical" (148). In each of the cases she undertakes, she sets out to seek the truth—not to cast any spells.

As the daughter of business tycoon Peter Strange, Violet lives a privileged life. The family home on Fifth Avenue is luxurious; she is driven about the city in a chauffeured limousine; she wears expensive clothes and is invited to select social events. Her younger brother, Arthur, is supportive of Violet's efforts but he does not have personal financial assets to help her. Consequently, even though she comes from a wealthy family, Miss Strange has to work covertly in order to acquire the funds she so desperately seeks. And though she is often repulsed by the sights she must investigate and plagued by nightmares, she continues to accept cases until she reaches her monetary goal.

"The Golden Slipper," the first problem that Violet solves, sets the tone for the collection. She is asked by the father of a young debutante to find out if his daughter is the compulsive thief responsible for a series of missing items. As the girl's reputation is at stake, it is crucial that Miss Strange maintain strict confidentiality, and that her presence in the midst of that select society not be suspect in any way. Because Violet Strange is a member of New York society's inner circle, she is readily accepted. And the fact that she is small and unassuming makes her appear to be non-threatening. While socializing with the suspect and her friends, Miss Strange observes the girl and the situation carefully. Her detectival method is scientific: she makes no assumptions; she gathers evidence, analyzes it, and makes a judgment. Often, as in this case, she sets up a trap for the guilty party. This time it is a Parisian dye which she sprinkles on selected lure—when the thief unknowingly gets it on her hands, Strange's reputation is established.

Although each case differs, basically Violet Strange's method of dealing with the puzzle is consistent. She uses both induction and deduction. There is nothing "feminine" about her thinking process: she approaches each situation as a mathematical problem. She also establishes a reputation for handling certain kinds of cases—theft and the location of lost articles, the prevention of crime and imminent scandal, the establishment of rightful heirs to property, and the investigation of past crimes to uncover the truth and free the innocent.

In locating lost articles, Miss Strange relies on her acute inductive faculties as well as on common sense. For example, in "The Dreaming Lady," the elderly sister of a financier who has just died has misplaced her brother's will. If it is not located, the family will be dispossessed and the home will be taken over by a n'er-do-well nephew. One of the unusual features of the case is the woman's sleepwalking—she put the will away on one of her nightly trips, but cannot remember where. Miss Strange assesses the situation carefully, accounts for the woman's daily routine, and locates the document.

In such cases, usually misfortune awaits a potential victim if the item is not found. A young widow will lose her husband's insurance annuity if it cannot be proven that he did not commit suicide. "The Second Bullet" recounts this problem. If Violet can find the second bullet that was allegedly fired the night George Hammond was shot, the case for suicide will be defeated and a young woman will not suffer infamy and financial ruin. Examination of the scene of the crime and accurate deductions lead Violet to the bizarre location of the second bullet. But perhaps the most bizarre location of a missing item is recounted in "Page Thirteen." While tracing the whereabouts of a page missing from a scientific report, Strange comes face to face with the skeletons in a famous family's secret closet. Through mathematical calculations, Violet determines that the paper must have dropped off the desk in the library and slipped under the wainscoting of a sealed door. She then crawls through a dank, narrow passage to retrieve the missing page. Usually she is faced with a cerebral task, but on occasions like this she also has to muster heroic physical as well as moral strength.

In several cases, Miss Strange is asked to solve a murder. "An Intangible Clue" demands that she discover at the scene of a brutal murder the significant clue that will lead to the identity of the killer. The police have combed the scene but have overlooked evidence that Violet discovers leading to the location of an unlikely witness to the crime. In "The House of Clocks" her task is more complex. Here she is called upon to prevent a murder, but uncovers a past murder instead. Once she assesses the plight of the young woman whose life is in danger, Violet places herself in the house posing as a nurse. She carries her nursing duties off well, while still managing to protect the woman and catch the guilty party. "The Doctor, His Wife, and the Clock" is a problem with similar features—a hidden crime which takes its toll upon a husband and wife. Miss Strange is asked to analyze a series of events which have puzzled the police. She is given a written account of the case as the basis for her evaluation. By following each of the events in a logical sequence and by making connections which others have overlooked, Violet Strange uncovers the truth.

Running through the series of problems is the thread of romance. After Roger Upjohn approaches Miss Strange with a delicate personal problem, a relationship develops between them. "The Grotto Spectre" recounts the disasterous marriage of Upjohn and the violent death of his wife by unknown hands. To quell the suspicion which has plagued the family since this occurrence, Upjohn hires Violet. She returns to the scene of the crime and sets up a trap for the murderer. By dressing up like the murdered woman and acting out the events as she has reconstructed them from witnesses to the crime, she elicits the angry response of the murderer. Her talent for impersonation works too well when she puts her own life on the line as she snares the guilty party. From this point on, Roger Upjohn becomes part of Violet Strange's life.

Finally, "Violet's Own" tells all. Upjohn has proposed marriage to her and she has accepted, and now he is to know her secret. A disowned older sister is the object of her concern—a woman who married an "outsider" considered inappropriate by her father. Violet has rescued her sister from penury and supported her blossoming singing career. Though the hope of reconciliation with their father is suggested, Violet is the only member of the family who reaches out to her.

Though Green married Violet Strange off and retired her from the work of detection, Violet made her mark. The match between Violet and Roger Upjohn is a likely one—both have suffered through trials, and respect the tenacity of the other. Violet demonstrates that a woman, even a young and privileged one, is capable of heady and gutsy work. Her detectival method indicates a talent for logic and mathematical puzzles, disproving the on-going notion that females are all heart. Despite Green's marrying her off, Violet rises above the stereotype of the helpless girl; she is empowered not by her marriage but rather by her intelligence and moral stealth.

The detective was for Green a heroic human being—not a physically powerful person, but an individual of moral power. Not one of her detectives ever abuses suspects; none carries a weapon. But they all have feet of clay: Gryce has his odd stare and rheumatism; Butterworth is nosey; Sweetwater is awkward; Strange has personal problems. Readers could easily relate to them. Of Green's detectives, Ebenezer Gryce and Amelia Butterworth are her most credible characters, probably because they are based on people Green knew. Gryce was like her own father, and Butterworth may have been based on one of the older women in her family. Readers trusted and admired Green's serial detectives, avidly following their adventures. Thus Green set the standard for future American fictional detectives.

Chapter Six
Sin and Crime

Anna Katharine Green does not portray psychopathic killers or perverted souls forced by circumstance or environment into a life of crime—she places the blame for crime on self-centeredness motivated by pride or greed. Nor does she portray wrong-doers as incapable of change and growth—instead, she presents characters as individuals, including those who overcome their weaknesses as well as those who do not. In an article entitled "Why Human Beings Are Interested in Crime," Green presents her views on criminal behavior: "...the great truth I have learned through my study of crime and its motives is that evil qualities are inevitably those which center in Self" (86). While noting that scientific inventions have brought change, Green contends that people are essentially the same, that "character remains the same—built of the eternal qualities of good and evil" (86). Her fiction reflects not only a focus on character, but also a religious orientation that specifically identifies sin as the cause of crime and grace as a force in establishing harmony. Intrinsic to the development of her stories are "providence," "grace," and "regeneration"—basic elements in Calvinistic theology. These elements distinguish her fiction from that of other writers of detective fiction, linking her works to the Puritan tradition.

A devout Presbyterian, Green's values are fleshed out in fictional characters who embody her social consciousness and religious convictions. Basic to her values is Calvinism transmitted through the New England Puritan tradition. From the arrival of her ancestors in the Massachusetts Bay Colony in the mid-Seventeenth Century, her family had been staunch church-goers. Her parents were married in the Second Presbyterian Church of Albany; she was baptized at Henry Ward Beecher's Plymouth Church in Brooklyn, where her parents were affiliated.[1] After she and Charles Rohlfs were married at the South Congregational Church in Brooklyn, she and her husband moved to Buffalo where they joined the First Presbyterian Church.[2] There they were assigned pew #73, which they held for more than forty years; yet they were more than church-goers for each participated in the communal mission of their congregation. Charles Rohlfs became a ruling elder (1890-93), while Anna served on various social action committees including the Women's Educational and Industrial Union, the Charity Organization Society, and the Volunteer Church Mission. Appropriately, her most famous female sleuth, Amelia Butterworth, is characterized as a woman of "strict Presbyterian training." And Ebenezer Gryce, though not specifically labelled, reflects the values of Puritan forebears.

Fiction became the means for Green to champion goodness and condemn evil. She was not alone in this endeavor, for changing social standards after the Civil War spawned a nationalistic effort, particularly among the middle class, to avert the erosion of American ideals. Crime, according to Davis, was viewed by many American writers as a "betrayal of a pure and noble heritage" (251). Green was among those writers who supported traditional American values. Her focus is almost exclusively American: her heroes and heroines, their life struggles, their values reflect the American experience. In her study, *The Feminization of American Culture*, Ann Douglas indicates that clergymen and middle-class literary women "attempted to stabilize and advertise in their work the values that cast their recessive position in the most favorable light.... They were Christians reinterpreting their faith as best they could is terms of the needs of their society" (10). Thus Green, like other writers who considered themselves Christian witnesses, assumed the responsibility for bringing cautionary messages to the public.

Despite a seemingly conventional life, Green had personal experiences that stimulated her social consciousness. When she was growing up, her family moved frequently—from city to village, from Manhattan to upstate New York, and back to Manhattan. Young Anna had a secure family, but she did not live the sheltered lifestyle of many other girls of her social class. Typically, New England-bred attorneys like her father set up practice in a community and stayed there, becoming part of an elite social group. However, the family's mobility gave her the opportunity to observe differences and to assert her own values. Later as the wife of Charles Rohlfs, she was in touch with various segments of society in her roles of wife, mother, and professional writer. She also maintained a wide range of contacts, corresponding with other writers as well as with friends and relatives.

Through the speech and actions of her characters, Green gives testimony to those beliefs which directed her own life. One can see the difference in the motivation of Green's characters and those of her peers in detective fiction. For example, Poe's M. Dupin, Le Blanc's Arsene Lupin, and Doyle's Sherlock Holmes use their superior intelligence to outwit criminal foes. While "chance" enters into the solution occasionally, for Dupin, Lupin, and Holmes, no supernatural intervention is suggested. However, Green's fiction recounts the operation of providence, grace, and regeneration. This well-defined Puritan strain runs through the entire Green canon, but is more dominant in some stories than in others. For example, Ebenezer Gryce evaluates clues and makes judgments like Dupin or Lupin, but he also is influenced by "providence" and assesses whether or not offenders are "repentant" of their crimes. And the denouement of *The Leavenworth Case* requires Mary Leavenworth to repent for the lies that have injured her character and to reject her uncle's fortune as a form of moral restitution. In Green's romances, the Puritan influence is more obvious than in her detective stories; selected here for discussion are works ranging from the more subtle to the most expressive, from the detective story to the romance.

The Mill Mystery (1886), a detective story, focuses on hidden crime, guilt, and the need for redemption. Constance Sterling, whose best friend has died of a broken heart after her fiance's suicide, assumes the role of amateur sleuth to find out what happened. She uncovers the tragic story of David Barrows, the young minister who was engaged to her friend. Called to the bedside of a dying man who had "an act of reparation to make," (258), Barrows found himself unwittingly involved in a family scheme to thwart the old man's last request. Samuel Pollard tried to protect the rights of an unacknowledged granddaughter. Barrows decoded a cypher in the man's prayerbook in order to locate the girl and protect her from harm—but he was neither bold nor quick enough to deal with his adversaries. Thus he blamed himself when the girl died: "When the hour of trial came, I failed to sustain myself, failed ignominiously, showing myself to be no stronger than the weakest of my flock.... I feared to lose my life, therefore my life must go. Nothing short of this would reinforce me in my own eyes, or give to me repentence that stern and absolute quality which the nature of my sin imperatively demands" (243). Barrows, overcome by guilt, isolated himself, prayed, engaged in self-flagellation, broke his engagement to be married, and finally took his own life. But suicide is clearly not the answer. For Constance Sterling (and the reader) the issue is only resolved when the guilty parties are brought to justice. Green treats the Reverend Barrows' suicide as a loss; she counters his actions with those of the resilient young woman, Constance Sterling, whose undaunting search for the truth prevails over Barrows' guilt. The heroine, a "sterling" character of "constant" virtue, is more than an amateur sleuth; she is a role model for the active Christian.

In *The Millionaire Baby* (1905), Green shows through the character of Dr. Pool how guilt can be re-directed into positive action. The narrator describes Pool as having been "calm and cold and, while outwardly scrupulous, capable of forgetting his honor as a physician under sufficiently strong temptation" (69). When challenged about his role in the disappearance of a young girl,

Pool responds: "That was Doctor Pool unregenerate and more heedful of the things of this world than of those of the world to come. You have to deal with quite a different man now. It is of that very sin I am now repenting in sackcloth and ashes. I live but to expiate it" (90). Pool's reparation takes the form of adopting a cast-away boy who responds to the attention Pool gives him. (As providence takes a mysterious turn for the old doctor, the reader gets a sense of the intensity of Calvinistic belief operating in the novel.)

The Puritan influence is particularly striking in a novel in which Green transforms a bizarre news report into a study of spiritual regeneration. In this novel, *Dr. Izard* (1895), Green presents a portrait of an enigmatic figure—a physician distinguished professionally, but a loner without family and close friends. The mystery of his character is heightened by the environment of his home—at the edge of a graveyard, placing him nearer the dead than the living. A hidden deed has cut him off from society and caused him to become increasingly reclusive. Once an affable young man engaged to be married, he now leads a monastic existence. The engagement was broken by him without explanation and all affective ties were cut.

Izard's only vital link with society is Polly Earle, an orphan girl whose parents were once close friends of his. Ever since her mother's death and her father's disappearance, Izard has helped to support the girl, even to setting up a trust fund for her future. Despite his distance, she grows up to respect him and look upon him as a father. Polly is a rosy-cheeked innocent who is too perfect to be human, and appears to be more a symbol than a flesh and blood girl.

When an imposter comes to town claiming to be Ephraim Earle, Polly's long lost father, life takes a turn for Izard. He knows the man is an imposter, but he cannot reveal the fact without confessing his own guilt. In a dramatic confessional scene, Izard repudiates his sin: "God forgive me that I have kept this deed a secret from you so long" (262). He reveals that after the death of Huldah Earle,

Polly's mother, he wanted to perform an autopsy to determine the cause of her illness, explaining that it was "the natural wish of so young and ambitious a man" (262). However, Ephraim Earle, not wanting his wife's body desecrated by an autopsy, refused to give permission. An overpowering desire to acquire scientific evidence of her malady led Izard to dig up the body in defiance of the husband. In the dark of the night as Dr. Izard was lifting the coffin, an enraged Ephraim Earle leapt upon him and he struck back in self-defense. In the fray, he killed Earle, but to cover up the deed he placed the husband in the wife's coffin and buried the wife in the cellar of his own house. Although he knew the crime was "involuntary," Izard hid the body so that his career would not suffer from the scandal. Green recounted that her nephew sent her a newspaper clipping about an Illinois doctor who became the basis for the character of Dr. Izard. In the actual case, however, the doctor left his confession to be read *after* his death ("AKG Tells How She Manufactures Her Plots" 48). In shaping the novel, Green drew upon Calvinistic theology to develop a character who comes to terms with his guilt *during* his lifetime; she intensifies his suffering and highlights the isolation which he endures in order to show how crime (sin) affects the human psyche. The novel, while not as successful as Green's detective fiction, maintains a balance between mystery and melodrama.

The "self" which Green identified as the cause of crime is also the basis for sin. According to Calvinistic belief, sin occurs when "God-centeredness becomes self-centeredness" (Leitch 38). Dr. Izard's ambition, his pursuit of his own scientific research at the cost of others, becomes his downfall. His regeneration requires more than recompensing Polly Earle for her loss. He must also go through a form of confession called justification. Justification is "an act of God's grace...an event," according to Calvinistic theology (Leitch 64). By publicly admitting his wrongful act, he is now able to reenter the community as a just man.

Elements of Izard's story are reminiscent of Nathaniel Hawthorne's *The Scarlet Letter.* (Green knew and admired Hawthorne's work; she also corresponded with Hawthorne's daughter, Rose Hawthorne Lathrop.)[3] Dr. Izard, like the Reverend Arthur Dimmesdale, is a respected man who suffers in secret from the effects of hidden sin. Both express their alienation from society in psycho-dynamic terms: they shun all affective bonds. Polly, like Pearl, is the link with society and the medium for grace. Justification occurs for both Dimmesdale and Izard at a communal gathering where each repudiates his sins and asks for forgiveness.

Another novel, *Dark Hollow* (1914), developed from a news report about a man who "does penance secretly, for twenty years, in a convict's cell of his own building in his house"; the house itself is "enclosed in a double tight board fence" ("Why Human Beings Are Interested in Crime" 84). Using these details as a basis, Green created the character of Judge Ostrander who allowed another man to be tried and executed for a crime that he himself committed. In fact, as the presiding judge, he sentenced the man. By imposing a convict-like existence upon himself, Ostrander thinks he can make amends for his double crime. "The seclusion sought was absolute"— no outsider has been seen entering the judge's house in years (3). Even his son, whom he loves dearly, has been sent away to school and has not even been home for holidays. Along with the social deprivation, the judge has set up an austere, prison-like environment in his home. A high, double fence surrounds the house. The judge's bedroom is as bare as a cell; his personal needs are met by a mute servant who is sworn to secrecy.

A resolution to the situation does not originate from Judge Ostrander. An outside force which Green calls "Providence"—a direct reference to the will of God—acts upon Ostrander. An innocent girl once again becomes the medium for change. Fortuitously, the grieving and the agrieved parties come together, forcing the judge to admit his hidden sin. With his confession comes the promise of a new beginning: renewed family ties, love, and peace of mind. "Crimes which are the result of sudden passion," according to Green, "are less interesting than premeditated ones, because real motive is lacking" ("Why Human Beings Commit Crimes" 84). Intellectual perversion, the thoughtful planning and execution of evil, is the controlling element in the development of the villain.

Green, like Hawthorne, perceives the most depraved man as one who misuses his intellectual gifts and victimizes the helpless or the most vulnerable. Orlando Brotherson of *Initials Only* (1911) is such a character. Juxtaposed against Orlando is his twin brother, Oswald. Although identical physically, they are opposites spiritually. Orlando is brilliant, capable of playing many roles, creative, charismatic—yet totally selfish and without any concern for other human beings. Unfortunately, both brothers fall in love with Edith Challoner, a beautiful New York debutante. When she is found dead under mysterious circumstances, a tale of vengeance begins to emerge.

Orlando Brotherson is rejected by Edith Challoner; he then determines that his brother will not have her either. A Cain and Abel motif develops as Orlando works out his cunning plan. He has killed before, just to see if a murder could be carried out to look like an accident. His first victim is a young washerwoman, whom he considers insignificant. Later, Edith Challoner is killed in a similar manner—with an icycle that pierces her heart. Consequently, no weapon is found, which is a problem for the detective; but the method is also the symbolic: "a bullet of ice for a heart of ice" (342). Orlando coldly explains his motivation to the father of the dead woman: "I did it because I regarded her treatment of my suit as insolent....I hated her for it; I hated her class, herself and all she stood for. To strike the dealer of such a hurt I felt to be my right. Though a man of small beginnings and of stock which such as you call common, I have a pride which few of your blood can equal" (341-342). Orlando Brotherson's pride leads to his downfall, for despite his remarkable invention, he has lost the respect of the community. His fame tainted by his evil deeds, he feels that not even Satan will want his company. In this novel, Green created one of her most depraved murderers.

"The House in the Mist" (1913) is not a detective story, but rather a parabolic short story which combines mystery and morality. On the surface, it is a tale of the haunted house variety, melodramatic and cautionary. Relatives are invited to the isolated house of Anthony Westonhaugh to have supper and hear his last will and testament. Before Westonhaugh's lawyer reads the will, he asks that any member of the nine people assembled leave the premises if he "feels, that for reasons he needs not state, he has no right to accept his share" (393). Eunice Westonhaugh, an unwed mother, relinquishes her claim: "I have sinned in the eyes of the world, therefore I cannot take my share of Uncle Anthony's money" (394). Her action pleases the remaining relatives since their shares will now be increased. However, in his testament, Westonhaugh accuses those present of causing the death of his wife by neglect and the death of his two children by direct acts of violence. Finally, the testament reveals that in order to gain his fortune, these relatives gave Westonhaugh poisoned wine, thus causing his slow death. At the same time the document discloses that the very same wine has already been served to the group present for the reading of the will and that within minutes each of them will die.

The story combines folk and Biblical motifs to produce a modern parable. Green introduces the narrator of the story as a young man seeking to make a new life for himself: "Being young, untrammelled, and naturally indifferent to danger, I was not averse to adventure; and having my fortune to make, was always on the lookout for Eldorado, which to ardent soul lies ever beyond the next turning" (369). He is "led" by providence to the house when he sees "a light shimmering through the mist" and follows it, though the "path toward the light was by no means an easy one" (369). Unwittingly, he is drawn into the drama unfolding before him as Anthony Westonhaugh's heirs are indicted and executed for their crimes. Thus in "seeking the light," he bears "witness" to the horror of evil. And although a stranger, he befriends the homeless and destitute Eunice Westonhaugh. Her fortune is reversed, however, when the lawyer announces: "Your withdrawal from the circle of heirs did not take from you your rightful claim to an inheritance which, according to your uncle's will, could be forfeited only by a failure to arrive.... "He made these arrangements to save from the general fate such members of his miserable family as fully recognized their sin and were truly repentant" (427). Both Eunice Westonhaugh and the young stranger are physically and spiritually renewed by the experience as they set off together, "two wayfarers still!" (428).

The image of the wayfarer or pilgrim is commonly used to signify the righteous Christian seeking salvation (like Christian in Bunyan's *Pilgrim's Progress*). On a purely moral level, the young "seeker" is reminiscent of the naive hero of Hawthorne's "My Kinsman Major Molineux" who, in witnessing the disgrace of his kin, attains a painful self-awareness. For the reader, the story provides an ageless lesson in the dangers of greed and the ravages of sin. As a final deterrent, Green paints a Dante-esque picture of the condemned evil-doers:

It was an awful moment. A groan, in which was concentrated the despair of seven miserable souls, rose from that petrified band; then, man by man, they separated and fell back, showing on each weak or wicked face the particular passions which had driven them into crime and made them the victims of this wholesale revenge. There had been some sort of bond between them till the vision of death arose before each shrinking soul. Shoulder to shoulder in crime, they fell apart as their doom approached, and rushing, shrieking, each man for himself, they one and all sought to escape by doors, windows or any outlet which promised release from this fatal spot. One rushed by me...and I felt as if a flame from hell had licked me, his breath was so hot and the moans he uttered so like the curses we imagine to blister the lips of the lost (421).

The description leaves no doubt as to the fate of the evil-doers. Its explicit condemnation of "the lost" is as "Puritan" as a Jonathan Edwards' sermon.

Green's position on crime is consistent. She perceives crime as a form of evil, originating from a weakness in character— selfishness that produces anti-social behavior. But she also explores the effects of such behavior, the psycho-dynamics of guilt and isolation. Basically, Green's position is Calvinistic. While her detective fiction contains subtle elements of Calvinism, her mystery stories, such as "The House in the Mist," are more explicit. In all of her fiction, however, her values distinguish Green from other writers of detective fiction and also place her within the American Puritan tradition and in the mainstream of American writers who focused on the threat to American ideals.

Chapter Seven
Women's Rights and Roles

As a college-educated, professional writer whose income exceeded that of her husband, Anna Katharine Green was the kind of woman to be supportive of women's causes. On the other hand, she was also middle-class, church-going, and family-oriented. The fact is that she wrote to Elihu Root in 1913 voicing her opposition to the women's suffrage movement (AKG: Letters). In examining her position today, Green's experience and her work seem to present contradictions. As Mrs. Charles Rohlfs, she played a conservative role for, like many other women of her social class, the stability of the home and family was her primary concern. At the same time, her fiction is embedded with messages advocating women's rights.

The majority of middle-class women who did not support the suffrage movement, according to Crumpacker, believed in "the ideal of a stable society based on appropriate power for men and women in their separate spheres" (78). Green exhibits the characteristics Crumpacker describes: she wrote about the problems of women and deplored injustice, but her approach was different from that of the suffragettes. In fact, as Mrs. Charles Rohlfs, she led an exceptionally quiet life writing, raising three children, and caring for her house and garden. To all appearances, she was a daughter of the nineteenth century—even her clothes reflected a lingering preference for Victorian fashions.[1] Yet her fiction clearly exposes inequities in the treatment of women and suggests reform. Green objected to the *style* of the suffragettes—a reaction common among people of her generation.

A case in point was the plight of Elizabeth Tilton, an advocate of women's rights, the wife of a Brooklyn editor, and a member of the Reverend Henry Ward Beecher's congregation at Plymouth Church. The Reverend Beecher was charged by Edward Tilton with the seduction of his wife Elizabeth. A trial which ran from January through June of 1875 played to a packed courtroom and received international publicity. In his study of the case, Robert Shaplen points out that the public was outraged that scandal should touch the Reverend Beecher, blaming Tilton's radical thinking for her downfall (13). The fact that Beecher was acquitted and then continued to draw thousands to his pulpit, while Tilton was ostracized and spent the remainder of her life in seclusion, reveals public distrust of radical social change. Shaplen contends that the verdict dramatized the American attitude toward female reformers: "...There was a narrow line in the minds of most Americans between what constituted 'vile women' and visionary reformers who seized upon the expansiveness of the times to demand more freedom in general for women" (13).

Anna Katharine Green's socialization defined specific roles for men and women. Baptized by the Reverend Beecher at Plymouth Church, she retained a life-long affiliation with the Presbyterian church. The daughter of Puritan-bred, New England parents, she was brought up according to patriarchal tradition in a home dominated by her father. As Mary Ryan points out in *The Empire of Mother*, "one of the most significant and pervasive structures" in the nineteenth century was the gender system (8). Writing became a means for Green to voice her concerns. She was not a "reformer" in the sense that she was part of a national movement, but she had definite ideas about gender roles. Green knew personally the oppression of paternal domination, especially in the constraints placed upon her creativity in having to write her first novel covertly in order not to incur her father's disapproval. In his study of Green's fiction, John Cornillon observes that she represents fathers as "repressive" (208). An analysis of Green's fictional world reveals a decided focus on families overpopulated with fathers, orphaned children, widows and widowers. The domination of fathers in Green's stories becomes a burden to sons as well as daughters and wives, but women tend to suffer more because of their economic dependence.

The society that Green portrays is patriarchal. Men are in positions of leadership in the community and in the family. Daughters and sons or nieces and nephews pay homage to a father-figure who determines whom they marry and how they live their lives. For example, a father-figure dominates Green's first two novels: in *The Leavenworth Case* (1878), two cousins are the wards of an uncle whose disapproval of a suitor leads to subterfuge and potential disgrace; *A Strange Disappearance* (1880) pivots on the terms of the inheritance a son receives from his widower father. The pattern is repeated in story after story. While not all fathers are despotic, the threat of exclusion from the family or disinheritance ensures parental control. While there are a few instances of mothering, no matriarchs play decisive roles, yet there are repeated occasions of "sisterly" support among women.

The ideal man in the Green canon is a protector of women. If not a knight in shining armor, he is expected to be strong and honorable. The male role model is also truly American in character—recognized as a success through his work, his wealth, and his good name. The Protestant ethic prevails—a self-made man is all the better. With pioneer spirit, adventurous young men prove their mettle by making their own fortunes. According to Joyce Warren in *The American Narcissus*, "While the American woman has been conditioned to accept unreal restrictions on her abilities, the American man has been encouraged to believe he is all powerful" (11). Consequently, while the marriageable female is characterized by innocence, lack of experience, and reliance upon family, the marriageable male is worldly-wise, hard-working, and success-oriented—a man willing and able to take care of a wife. The system fails when excessive ambition or greed motivates a man to gain through illegal means such as murder, theft, larceny, impersonation, bigamy, or abandonment of wife and family. Once a man fails to maintain his social contract, his fiancee or wife is the likely victim.

By focusing on cultural constraints that place women in vulnerable situations, Green voiced her protest. If, as Crumpacker suggests, the "activity" of female characters reflects the author's position, then Green might be considered a "domestic feminist"— one who believes in "women's stabilizing power within a developing society" (79, 78). Among female characters in the Green canon, power is a significant characteristic. As Warren points out, "...the most significant aspect of women's status in nineteenth-century America was their powerlessness (9)." Women who lack power are the most likely victims, and women who are self-empowered are heroic as well as successful. Although Green depicts weak as well as strong women, her most admirable females are those who are self-assertive, often challenging authority figures to seek the truth or redress wrongs.

By the very nature of their activity, female sleuths step out of the conventional role, wresting power—if necessary. Prime examples are Amelia Butterworth and Violet Strange, whose activities, as we have seen in Chapter Five, distinguish them from other women of their generation. Amelia Butterworth, though wealthy and socially secure, engages in police work—an activity considered unfeminine. Yet, she does not repudiate her position in society nor does she reject her gender role. In working with Inspector Gryce, Butterworth uses her brains and her insight into human behavior to solve crime, but she does not aspire to trade places with him. Instead she assumes a protective stance with women who have been victimized, becoming nurse, psychologist, mother, sister, friend as the need arises. Like Green herself, Amelia Butterworth is far from the conventional Gramercy Park "lady," but not quite the suffragette.

In contrast, Violet Strange is more radical than Butterworth. She defies her father, enters the seamy world of the private investigator and sells her talent. As one critic observes,"...although Violet upholds the myth in public by conforming to the role expected of a young woman of her station in life, it is a hollow act, and in secret she lives a life in defiance of those role expectations" (Cornillon 208). Like Butterworth, she is operative "outside" of her own home in her efforts to maintain or restore harmony to the lives of clients. As her name implies, Violet is small and delicate physically, but she is still capable of shouldering enormous intellectual and social burdens, using her powers to assist both males and females. The inference is clear that women have ability and strength, even though they have neither the political nor the physical clout of men. Both women are "movers" and "restorers"—strong, daring, and different from typical females of their station. It is this assertion of female power within the traditional setting that makes Green a "domestic feminist."

The sources for Green's female characters are likely to have come from experience and from newspaper accounts of real-life situations. Habegger points out that "...character-types in fiction often appear to be versions of available gender roles in the reader's culture" (ix). Green's characters were recognizable to her readers, for these characters represented certain cultural types—single females, widows, married women. In fact, as Habegger asserts, "...readers, especially adolescent girls,...(had cause) to think out with the help of book-length narrative the potential life-consequences of being a given kind of woman" (ix). Consequently, the plight of fictional characters such as Green's was often a social commentary—not simply a means to reveal a mystery or to entertain. Green's fiction reflects an awareness of the status of women, from youth to old age, within a range of societal structures.

The innocent girl was viewed by nineteenth-century society as a means through which the worldly man would find goodness and harmony. " 'Goodness,' " according to Calder, "required a home, a wife, children, and servants. It needed a door to shut against temptation, corruption and threat" (14-15). In "The Hermit of— Street" (1900), for example, Green projects an urban allegory of the innocent girl. Delight Hunter, a country girl, visits her aunt in New York City and is promptly captivated by a man who lives next door. She marries him, moves into his house but is forbidden access to the top floor. Eventually she discovers that her husband has made a prisoner of his employer, Mrs. Ransome, in order to use her monetary resources. The story has aspects of a parable with its charactermimic names and moralistic tone. The theme is reinforced by the young wife's reaction to her husband's deception: "Though I can never look upon my husband with the frank joy I see in other women's faces, I have learned not to look upon him with distrust, and to thank God I did not forsake him when desertion might have meant the destruction of one small seed of goodness which had developed in his heart with the advent of a love for which nothing in his whole previous life had prepared him" (343-344). The characterization of Delight Hunter as a Patient Grizelda is obviously drawn from the myth of the "saintly" girl. In his study of the period, Eaken describes the "redemptive" role of women as "one of the most characteristic phenomena of nineteenth-century American novels" (5). In discussing the conditioning of nineteenth-century women, Delight Hunter's story makes a good case for Fetterley's thesis in *The Resisting Reader*, that "immasculation" (the process by which women accept male myths about women) influenced even female authors, like Green, to project such myths (xx). Yet, the tale is moderated by the fact that Delight Hunter is patient but not passive: when she discovers the truth, she takes charge by releasing Mrs. Ransome and then making a deal to save her husband, thus proving herself to be both an arbitrator and an activist.

The future of the young, single female in the nineteenth century depended on how well she could marry or, if she were to remain single, how willing and able her parents or siblings were to support her. Economics was often the bottom line in determining a woman's future. In *The Mill Mystery* (1886), Green is more assertive about the need for female independence as seen in the situations of the main characters in the novel. Two women are without families to support them: Ada Reynolds dies of a broken heart after the death of her fiance; her friend, Constance Sterling, is on the brink of despair because she has no opportunities for self-support. The narrator explains: "Oh, the deep sadness of a solitary woman's life! The sense of helplessness that comes upon her when every effort made, every possibility sounded, she realizes that the world has no place for her, and that she must either stoop to ask the assistance of friends or starve!" (5-6). Single women without family were most vulnerable, for even the seemingly advantaged did not determine their own futures. Respectable employment opportunities for females were limited by the popular misconception that work labelled a woman less feminine and less socially desirable. "The urban middle and upper-classwoman on the eastern seaboard," according to Warren, "was restricted by the conventional image of the lady" (9). Green attempts to change this popular attitude through her characterization of Constance Sterling, the heroine of *The Mill Mystery* who proclaims to a prospective suitor, "I am no longer ashamed to own that I stand by myself, and work for every benefit I obtain" (105). Representing a new generation of enlightened young men, he responds: "Nor need you be.... In this age and in this country a woman like yourself forfeits nothing by maintaining her own independence. On the contrary, she gains something, and that is the respect of every true-hearted man that knows her" (105). Constance Sterling's determination to make a life for herself offered a model for male as well as female readers.

Green was well aware of the struggles of the working woman. Ever since her graduation from college she had continued to write and seek sources for publication. But her elder sister, Sarah Elizabeth Green, provided an intimate study. Miss Green lived in a rooming house at 37 Monroe Place in Brooklyn, New York, supporting herself through sewing long hours for special customers. She described her situation in a letter to Anna dated May 22, 1891: "I have so many things which trouble me. Today I ought to have seen three people and none came. One owes me money. Mrs. Lyman Abbott wants to talk about some work, and the other lady I am making shirt clothes for her baby and should have had a call from her. All these disappointments will put back the work, they won't like that" (AKG: Letters). The same letter reveals that Anna and her brother Sidney were contributing to her support: "I do appreciate your money and Sidney's, yours is kept for the weekly rent. Last month most of Sidney's went into glasses, in a new pair of spectacles and one new glass in the eye glasses." Sarah Elizabeth Green was thirteen years older than her sister and, as the eldest in the family, helped to raise her four siblings when their mother died. She had not received any training other than the skills learned in the home— typical of women of her generation. Until her death, she had to depend on the generosity of relatives to sustain herself.

The work a middle class, single woman could find was so limited that many found themselves in the position of the "genteel poor." Green discloses in her stories how mercenary guardians could take advantage of young women who had no control over their own fortunes. In *The Mill Mystery*, a daughter is unwillingly married off to a British lord who only wants her dowery—her parents, however, care only for the title that this marriage will bring to their family. A grand-daughter, the child of a ne'er do well son, is kept hidden away, for her mere existence could bring scandal. Her grandmother, who wants no financial or social responsibility for the girl, puts her into the hands of a woman who runs a brothel where the girl commits suicide. In "The House of Clocks" (1915), the message, "I do not want to die," is inscribed on a sampler secretly transmitted to a visitor by a young girl. When Violet Strange enters the house disguised as a nurse, she discovers a teenaged girl who is virtually a prisoner in the home of her step-mother. Helene is finally rescued and the money to which she is entitled is restored.

Even if she were wealthy, a single woman had to have a respectable public image in order to be considered "marriageable." A man could be judged by his potential in his job or career, his presentation of self as a "manly" individual. But a marriageable female, as Tuttleton indicates in his study of the period, had "to have no past to conceal" (131). While a man's worldliness and experience were valued along with his financial and social assets, a woman's innocence was the crucial factor. In "Shall He Wed

Her" (1891), Green develops a cautionary tale, warning women and perhaps chiding men on the standard of female innocence. Because there is a shadow on her character, a suitor decides not to marry Mrs. Walforth, an attractive widow. As one of three women seen in the parlor of a downtown hotel where money was extorted, she is a suspect—but her guilt or innocence is never established. The issue is not brought to Mrs. Walforth; instead her suitor and his lawyer friend weigh the "risk" of marrying a woman with a "flaw" in her character. After the liason is broken, the narrator asks the reader if it was wrong to separate "two hearts whose right it was to be made happy" (202). Green, through the narrator, infers that the double standard hurts both men and women, that the consequences of being influenced by cultural pressure may jeopardize a person's happiness.

One of My Sons (1901) reveals how a father can dominate a son's life and that of his daughter-in-law—even to the point of forcing the girl into the streets. The elder Mr. Gillespie rejects his son's bride—a dancer—as unsuitable. Although Leighton Gillespie falls in love with Milles Fleurs and marries her despite his father's objections, he is not strong enough to defend her. His widower father maintains absolute control over the family finances; in fact, all of his sons still reside in the family mansion. If Leighton Gillespie is to survive, he has no choice but to live under his father's roof under his terms. Milles Fleurs, however, is a free spirit who is stifled by the rigidity of the family and chooses to leave husband and child rather than endure a lifetime of censure. In this novel, Green shows how the socio-economic system reinforced the power of the patriarch whose sons were tied to him less by filial devotion than by purse strings. The "inappropriate" girl wed to an heir to the family fortune either stayed in the home as a marginal (often abused) figure or she "ran away"—but without money she would have a hard life ahead of her, as the tragedy of Milles Fleurs reveals.

Even if a married woman was "appropriate" and had a sizable inheritance at her disposal, control over her resources was surrendered to her husband. Green illustrates the jeopardy in which property laws robbed women of their wealth in *The Step on the Stair* (1923). Aware that his daughter may lose the family fortune if she marries a man who cannot manage money, a father tries to find an honest husband for his daughter. He makes no attempt to educate his daughter in financial matters, for under the law her husband will control her assets. Consequently, the choice of the best man involves more than love and good intentions. Once married, a woman's lifestyle is determined by her husband. If he misuses funds or gambles, she might find herself in the situation of Mrs. L'Hommedieu, the pathetic figure in Green's short story, "The Gray Madam" (1900). Striving to maintain security after her husband has wasted all the money she brought to their marriage, Mrs. L'Hommedieu hides a bond that her husband threatens to use as collateral for gambling. Her anxiety builds to the breaking point when he loses, leaving her destitute and deranged. The story highlights a fact that shaped the destinies of many wives—that the vulnerability of women came not from feminine weakness, but from the lack of "economic" stability (Calder 17).

Green shows how easy it was for a man to leave town, put some distance between himself and his former life, and assume a new identity. Newspapers of the day regularly included accounts of missing persons and abandoned families. In his account of nineteenth century New York life, McCabe reports that the records of the Bureau for the Recovery of Lost Persons indicate that the disappearances of men was a serious problem—that thousands of men reported missing had never been found (848). Green knew personally of the case of a childhood friend whose husband left her and their children. In a letter dated 13 October 1891, Sarah Elizabeth Green wrote to her sister about their friend in East Haddam, Connecticut: "Jeannie's husband has left his wife and four little girls (and) run away..." (AKG: Letters). Cases such as this reveal the differences in the mobility and in the chances for success for men and women. Clearly, a woman left at home with the children was at the mercy of friends and family. But a man was reasonably free to move on and renegotiate his life, especially if he had marketable skills.

Green focused on women as likely victims of abandonment or bigamy in *That Affair Next Door* (1897), *The Mayor's Wife* (1907) and *The Mystery of the Hasty Arrow* (1917). While a woman's entire life was scrutinized by prospective suitors, the man was often accepted at face value. (It is significant to note that the fiction written after Green's marriage focuses more on the problems of married women.) In *That Affair Next Door* (1897), Green develops a mystery around the betrothal of a young debutante to a well-known man about town. She is genteel, innocent, and wealthy; he is handsome, suave, and attentive. On their wedding day, as the bride comes down the center aisle of a Fifth Avenue church, a second bride—heavily veiled—emerges from a side aisle. Revealing herself before the congregation, the second bride reports that she is the bridegroom's wife whom he married and abandoned years before. So well had the young man assumed his new identity that even the most discriminating among New York society suspected nothing of his past. The degree to which he would go to cover his tracks has led him to murder; the case demonstrates the vulnerability of women and the contrasting social mobility of men. McCabe points that there is "no city in the Union in which imposters of all kinds flourish so well as in New York" (316). Even people who should have known better were easily taken in, "but the women," according to McCabe, "are most frequently the victims" (317).

In *The Mystery of the Hasty Arrow*, Ermentrude Taylor is abandoned by Carleton Roberts when he is assured of a more profitable marriage which will offer him political advantages. "Married but not acknowledged" (409), Ermentrude seeks a life of her own, bearing his child secretly and then giving it up for adoption. She appears to have endured despite the ills of fortune, but Roberts suffers a tragedy before his ambitions are fully realized. Miss Taylor does not press for her rights because she is embarrassed by her predicament and has no proof of her marriage since fire destroyed the records. (Records of births and marriages, especially in rural areas, were not always entered accurately or preserved adequately.) In each of these novels, Green's treatment of bigamy reflects her condemnation of it, and of the man who abandons a woman in order to start life over again with a more profitable match. Desertion was common in the United States because it was relatively easy for a man to leave wife and children, debts and losses, and begin a new life elsewhere. It was not until social security listings and related systematic governmental record systems were established that individuals could not readily assume a new identity.

The situations of a man and a woman who have kept secret a legal first marriage, but have married a second time, are contrasted in *The Mayor's Wife* (1907). Olympia Packard is haunted by a man she married in haste and desperation as a young girl in Minnesota. Penniless and with no prospects for the future, she is cajoled into marrying John Brainard. Realizing her mistake just minutes after the ceremony, she flees from town. He threatens to kill himself, and she believes that he has carried out that threat. After she is adopted by a wealthy uncle, she marries Henry Packard, a successful politician who has since become mayor of the city. Another woman, Elizabeth Brainard, has been left by her husband to seek out an existence clerking in a small shop across from the mayor's home. Hopeful of his return, Mrs. Brainard says, "I am a married woman, Miss, and shouldn't be working like this. And I won't always; my man'll come back and make a lady of me again. It's that I'm waiting for" (170). Unknown to either of them John Silverthorn Brainard was married *to both* of them—but Bess is his first (and legal) wife. This is not discovered until he tries to blackmail Olympia Packard, threatening to reveal her past and ruin her husband's career. Green takes a strong position against Brainard and clearly sympathizes with the two women. She exonerates Olympia Packard by building a case for her youth and innocence, her desperation in a society which has no place for the girl who is without family. Elizabeth Brainard is depicted as a Patient Grizelda who bears abuse and rejection but still clings to her husband. Brainard is clearly the villain—an opportunist who uses women to achieve his ends (even his elderly aunts who raised him have not been spared.)

In her work, *Women as a Force in History*, Mary R. Beard traces "women's historic subjection" to Sir William Blackstone's *Commentaries on the Laws of England*. Blackstone's interpretation of marriage was carried over into American law: "By marriage, the husband and wife are one person in law; that is, the very being or legal existence of the woman is suspended during the marriage, or at least is incorporated and consolidated into that of the husband; under whose wing, protection, and cover, she performs everything..." (Beard 88-89). The suspension of "legal existence" placed women in a vulnerable position. Divorce was a complicated and expensive procedure as well as a social taboo until the turn of the century. At the same time marriage and a family was the primary value in society. Calder points out that "in Victorian fiction almost the whole of human life could in a sense be contained in the family...." (14). The risks were high, especially for women who had no escape from an unhappy union.

Green presents happy marital situations as well as unhappy ones; in fact, many of her stories have the proverbial happy ending. However, *Miss Hurd: An Enigma* (1894) describes the plight of a run-away wife—Mrs. Vashti Murdoch married to Thomas Murdoch, a wealthy California rancher. She has travelled from the west to the east coast, from New England to New York City in a vain attempt to escape from her husband. She disguises herself and takes whatever employment she can find, living in extreme poverty at times. Meanwhile, she is constantly tracked by Murdoch who declares, "she belongs to me" (28). Vashti Murdoch's reaction to being reclaimed is like that of an animal at bay: "Drawn up in the remotest corner in an attitude appalling to behold,...she had caught up a stick of rough wood from the neighboring fireplace and now stood with it brandished high over her head, in an attitude of threat and defiance which was almost titanic in its suggestion of concentrated power and passion" (29). A young woman of extraordinary beauty and bearing, Mrs. Murdoch is portrayed as a pathetic figure. Her husband is described as a calm, dark, powerful individual—an egotist who brooks no interference with his desires, who considers his wife's fight the result of "maddening caprices" (178). He perceives her as abnormal, motivated by "an almost masculine desire for independence" (205). The reader never becomes privy to the details of the couple's personal relationship—but in Murdoch's lack of understanding, his ill-tempered responses and reckless behavior, sadism is suggested. For example, at one point he purchases a sculpture of his wife and then smashes it. The gesture reflects his attitude toward his wife, perceiving her as a commodity which he owns and can destroy at will.

Although Green does not come out directly for the dissolution of this marriage, she depicts it as irreparable. She is quite explicit, however, in depicting the interaction between another couple in the same novel, a ranch hand and his abandoned wife. Susan confronts Jasper: " 'Am I not your wife?... Were we not married four years ago in Cheyenne....' For reply his hand came down. It struck her heavily, and she fell. He, with a sullen air...touched her with his foot. 'get up!' he cried. 'Don't make a fool of yourself because I forgot I had once promised to protect you.' " When he discovers he has killed her, he says, "She shouldn't have minded any such knock as that.... I have given as much or more to the horses often, and it makes them stand around" (328). The detailed account of this encounter contrasts with the veiled treatment of the Murdochs' relationship. This may well come down to social class, to the assumption that the lower class is likely to be physically abusive, while the upper class is given to more subtle forms of mistreatment. Green is explicit in her condemnation of the ranch hand, but she deals with Thomas Murdoch indirectly, ironically. It is fate rather than the law which releases Murdoch's hold on his wife. When the body of Susan, the murdered girl, is found; authorities think it must be Mrs. Murdoch's body. Thomas Murdoch is at the mercy of a lynch mob; his wife heroically gives up her freedom to come to his rescue—but he dies of fright. The reader sees some ambivalence here on Green's part. She portrays Thomas

Murdoch as a villain, his wife the victim of his abuse, the marriage broken—yet her religious beliefs and middle class values did not permit her to advocate divorce, at least not openly. Consequently, she contrives an ending which is not a solution to the problem, but rather the only way out for Vashti Murdoch—the death of the husband.

In reviewing the presentation of male and female roles in Anna Katharine Green's fiction, certain features emerge—a commitment to marriage, family, and respect for individual rights. Clearly, she does not reject men, or romance, or marriage. However, she decries the abuse of the weak by the strong and, most often, the "strong" are the people who have money and power—usually older males, frequently fathers or husbands. Women continued to be most likely victims because they had limited opportunities for self-support and virtually no protection of their personal assets in marriage. Although she did not offer specific solutions to the issues projected in her fiction, Green highlighted problems for public scrutiny. If, as Habbegar suggests, readers tried on the roles of characters presented in fiction (ix), then Green's message to men was to be honorable and considerate in their relationships with women; to women, Green offered the models of independent females who fought for their rights and were rewarded for their efforts.

Afterword

On April 11, 1935, at the age of eighty-eight, Anna Katherine Green died at her home in Buffalo, New York. She had lived a long and active life—she saw the United States develop from a young country divided during the Civil War, through the sweeping changes of industrialization and westward expansion, to a powerful nation. As daughter, wife, mother, grandmother, and professional writer, she recorded the American experience. She has to her credit thirty-five novels and twenty-three short stories, a volume of poetry, and a poetic drama, as well as a collection of unpublished plays.

Of all her literary efforts, her detective fiction was most successful, appearing at a time when the public was ready for literature that provided *solutions* to problems. And readers were (and still are) fond of literature in which man's rational and humanistic endeavors prevail. Green provided a compelling story and a challenging puzzle but, most of all, she created credible detectives. She captured the imagination of thousands of readers with the adventures of Ebenezer Gryce, Amelia Butterworth, Violet Strange, and a host of amateur sleuths. Her detectives are unique men and *women*—movers and shakers—whose common sense and unaffected demeanor distinguished them as Americans. One of the pioneers who shaped detective fiction into a vital form with its own conventions and integrity, Green became a mentor to the scores of writers who followed her in the genre. Assessing her contribution to American letters, Howard Haycraft writes, "...her plots are models of careful construction that can still hold their own against today's competition. For this quality, and by virtue of precedence and sustained popularity, she occupies an undisputed and honorable place in the development of the American detective story" (85).

But, Anna Katharine Green achieved more than simply the title "Mother of Detective Fiction." As the details of her career emerge, we see a professional writer—an American woman who single-mindedly pursued a literary career, despite the odds against her. Even though the literary establishment, as well as her own father, was not supportive of professional women writers, she worked diligently at her craft, producing fiction for over sixty years. The substance of her stories is the culture of antebellum America, especially the lifestyles of New Yorkers. From real-life situations, she wove tales of mystery and imagination that reveal the strengths and weaknesses of nineteenth century America, often focusing on the problems of the vulnerable, the likely victims. Her novels and short fiction reflect the concerns of her own generation—a people who had celebrated their centennial, whose experience was unique.

Notes

Foreword
Source

Murch, Alma E. *The Development of the Detective Novel.* Westport, Connecticut: Greenwood Press, 1981.

Chapter One
Notes

[1]See "Anna Katharine Green" [Obit.], *Publisher's Weekly,* 127, 20 April 1935, 1599.

[2]Green's father, James Wilson Green, had acquaintances on the police force, including at least one police chief. Green recalls trips to Long Island, sitting in the back seat of a carriage and listening to her father and the police chief converse in the front seat: see "Why Human Beings Are Interested in Crime," *American Magazine.* February 1919:39.

[3]Edith Wharton is an upperclass New York female writer of the period. Her novel *The Age of Innocence* (1900) offers an insider's view of a privileged society.

Sources

Bleiber, E.F., ed. Introduction. *Monsieur Lecoq.* New York: Dover, 1975.

Bragin, Charles. *Bibliography: Dime Novels 1860-1964.* Brooklyn: Miller Print Shop, 1964.

Collins, Wilkie. *The Critic,* 28 January 1893, p. 152.

Coultrap-McQuin, Susan M. "Why Their Success?" *Legacy,* 1 (Fall 1984): 1, 8-9.

Christie, Agatha. *An Autobiography.* New York: Dodd, Mead, 1977.

Davis, David Brion. *Homicide in American Fiction.* Ithaca, N.Y.: Cornell University Press, 1957.

Fetterley, Judith. *The Resisting Reader.* Bloomington: Indiana University Press, 1978.

Fiedler, Leslie. *Love and Death in the American Novel.* New York: Stein and Day, 1966.

Green, Anna Katharine. *The Leavenworth Case.* New York: George Putnam Sons, 1878.

Haycraft, Howard. *Murder for Pleasure.* New York: D. Appleton-Century, 1941.

Horton, Rod W. *Social and Individual Values in the New York Stories of Edith Wharton.* New York: New York University Press, 1948.

Lewis, R. W. B. *Edith Wharton.* New York: Harper and Row, 1975.

Longstreet, Stephen. *City on Two Rivers.* New York: Hawthorne Books, Inc., 1975.

Mott, Luther. *Golden Multitudes: The Stories of Best Sellers in the United States.* New York: Macmillan and Company, 1947.

Mann, Jessica. *Deadlier Than the Male.* New York: Macmillan Company, Inc., 1981.

Murch, Alma E. *The Development of the Detective Novel.* Westport, Conn.: Greenwood, 1981.

Nevins, Allan. *A History of the American People.* London: Oxford University Press, 1970.

Pearson, Edmund. *Dime Novels.* Port Washington, N.Y.: Kennikat Press, 1968.

Tuttleton, James W. *The Novel of Manners in America.* Chapel Hill: University of North Carolina Press, 1972.

Woodward, Kathleen. "Anna Katharine Green." *Bookman.* October 1929: 168-170.

Chapter Two

Notes

[1]For the family trees of the Green and Whitney families, see S.W. Phoenix, *The Whitney Family of Connecticut,* New York: Columbia University Press, 1878, I, 712-713; II, 1518.

[2]See *The Brooklyn Directory* 1847, 1848.

[3]See Phoenix, p. 1518, for places and dates.

[4]See *The New York Directory,* 1847-1850.

[5]For church membership records of JWG, see *A Church in History,* 1949 (centenary publication of Plymouth Church).

[6]See *The Commercial Advertiser Directory,* Buffalo 1857.

[7]See *Notable American Women* 1607-1950, II, 79.

[8]For a history of the college and a list of early graduates, see Green Mountain Junior College Catalog, Poultney, Vermont.

[9]Sarah Green's letter of 22 May 1891 thanks Anna and her husband for sending money and mentions that Sidney is also helping her (Letters: AKG).

[10]Sarah Green's letter of 22 May 1891 laments that Anna has bought land and decided to stay in Buffalo.

Sources

Clark, Robert Judson, et al. *The Arts and Crafts Movement in America.* Princeton: Princeton University Press, 1972.

Daly, Augustin. Letters (unpublished). Folger Library, Washington, D.C.

Daly, Joseph Francis. *Life of Augustin Daly.* New York: Macmillan, 1917.

Green, Anna Katharine. Letters (unpublished). Collection of Mary Alice Rohlfs.

———. *The Sword of Damocles.* New York: G.P. Putnam's Sons, 1909.

"A Little Known Husband," *The Literary Digest.* 29 May 1915, 1291.

Kindilien, Carlin. "Anna Katharine Green," *Notable American Women* 1607-1950, ed. James Jones et al. II, 79-80.

Maio, Kathleen L. "Anna Katharine Green Rohlfs," *American Women Writers,* Ed. Linda Mainero. New York: Frederick Unger Publishing Company, 1981. III, 498-500.

"Noted Buffalonians, Wed Half Century Ago, Happy," *Buffalo Courier Express,* 18 November 1934, 1-2.

"Plane Crash Victim Friend of Calles," *NYT,* 29 March 1928, 10.

"Rholse-Green," *Brooklyn Daily Eagle.* 26 November 1884, 15.

Rohlfs, Charles. Letters to AD (unpublished). Catalogued under Letters of Augustin Daly. Folger Library, Washington, D.C.

Rohlfs, Mary Alice. Interview. New York: 4 June 1979.

Walt Whitman's New York. Ed. Henry M. Christman. New York: Macmillan Company, 1963.

Weld, Ralph Foster. *Brooklyn Is America.* New York: Columbia University Press, 1950.

Chapter Three

Notes

[1]See advertisement reprinted inside the cover of *Risifi's Daughter* (1887).

[2]Uncollected Letters of Augustin Daly. Folger Library. Washington, D.C.

[3]Mary Alice Rohlfs recounted that Charles Rohlfs designed the original chafing dish (Interview, 6/4/79). One of Charles Rohlfs' clocks is among the collection of the Metropolitan Museum of Art, listed among 1986 acquisitions.

Sources

Emerson, Ralph Waldo. *The Letters of RWE.* Ed. R. L. Rusk. New York: Columbia University Press, 1939.

Gilbert, Sandra and Susan Gilbert. *The Mad Woman in the Attic.* New Haven: Yale University Press, 1979.

Green, Anna Katharine. "The Bronze Hand," "The House in the Mist, "Midnight at Beauchamp Row" and "Staircase at Heart's Delight" in *A Difficult Problem and Other Stories*. New York: F. P. Lupton Publishing Company, 1900. Reprinted New York: Garrett Press, 1969.

_____ *A Defence of the Bride and Other Poems*. New York: G. P. Putnam's Sons, 1882.

_____ *The Doctor, His Wife, and the Clock*. New York: G.P. Putnam's Sons, 1895.

_____ *The Forsaken Inn*. New York: R. Bonner's Sons, 1890. Reprinted Freeport, New York: Books for Libraries, 1971.

_____ *The House in the Mist*. Indianapolis: The Bobbs-Merrill Company, 1905.

_____ *The House of the Whispering Pines*. New York: G.P. Putnam's Sons, 1910.

_____ "The Little Steel Coils," "Room No. 3," in *Masterpieces of Mystery*. New York: Dodd, Mead and Company, 1912.

_____ *Marked Personal*. New York: G.P. Putnam's Sons, 1893.

_____ *Risifi's Daughter, A Drama*. New York: G.P. Putnam's Sons, 1887.

_____ *7 to 12* and *One Hour More*. New York: G.P. Putnam's Sons, 1887.

_____ *Three Thousand Dollars*. Boston: R.G. Badger, 1910.

_____ *To the Minute* and *Scarlet and Black*. New York: G.P. Putnam's Sons, 1916.

_____ *XYZ*. New York: G.P. Putnam's Sons, 1883.

McCabe, J.D. *Lights and Shadows of New York Life*. New York: Farrar, Straus and Giroux, 1970. Reprinted from the 1872 edition.

Rohlfs, Mary Alice. Interview. New York: 4 June 1979.

Walker, Cheryl. *The Nightingale's Burden: Women Poets* and *American Culture Before 1900*. Bloomington, Indiana: Indiana University, 1982.

Walling, George. *Recollections of a New York Chief of Police*. Montclair, New Jersey: Patterson Smith, 1972. Reprinted from the 1887 edition.

Wells, Carolyn. "Heart-to-Heart Talks with Authors," *The Critic*, 42 (May 1903): 467-468.

Chapter Four

Notes

[1]New York is the setting for most of Green's fiction although she used other locales including Vermont, Massachusetts, Connecticut, Pennsylvania, Washington D.C., Ohio, Chicago, New Mexico, and Colorado.

[2]For an evaluation of Charles Rohlfs' craft, see Robert J. Clark, *The Arts and Crafts Movement in America*. Princeton: Princeton University Press, 1972.

Sources

Cawelti, John D. *Adventure, Mystery and Romance.* Chicago: University of Chicago Press, 1976.

Champigny, Robert. *What Will Have Happened.* Bloomington: Indiana University Press, 1977.

Christie, Agatha. *An Autobiography.* New York: Dodd, Mead and Company, 1977.

Green, Anna Katharine. *Behind Closed Doors.* New York: G.P. Putnam's Sons, 1888.

———— *The Filigree Ball.* Indianapolis: Bobbs-Merrill Company, 1905.

———— *Hand and Ring.* New York: G.P. Putnam's Sons, 1883.

———— "The House in the Mist," "Staircase at Heart's Delight," "Midnight in Beauchamp Row" in *Masterpieces of Mystery.* New York: Dodd, Mead and Company, 1912.

———— *Lost Man's Lane.* New York: G.P. Putnam's Sons, 1898.

———— *One of My Sons.* New York: G.P. Putnam's Sons, 1901.

Mooney, Joan. "Best Selling American Detective Fiction," *The Armchair Detective,* 3 (January 1970): 98-113.

Nevins, Allan. *A History of the American People.* London: Oxford University Press, 1970.

Rinehart, Mary Roberts. *Miss Pinkerton.* New York: Rinehart and Company, 1959.

———— *My Story.* New York: Rinehart and Company, 1948.

Still, Bayard. *Mirror for Gotham.* New York: New York University Press, 1956.

Chapter Five

Notes

[1]The Police Commissioner to whom Green referred is likely to be either James Kelso or John Jourdan. Theodore Roosevelt who was Police Commissioner from 1895 to 1897 was also an acquaintance of Green's, but obviously Gryce appeared almost twenty years before Roosevelt assumed that position.

Sources

Green, Anna Katharine. *Agatha Webb.* New York: G.P. Putnam's Sons, 1899.

———— *The Circular Study.* New York: McClure, Phillips and Company, 1900. Reprinted: New York: Garland Publishing Company, 1976.

———— *The Doctor, His Wife, and the Clock.* New York: G.P. Putnam's Sons, 1895.

_____ *The Golden Slipper and Other Problems for Violet Strange*. New York: G.P. Putnam's Sons, 1915. Contents: "The Golden Slipper," "The Second Bullet," "The Intangible Clew," "The Grotto Spectre," "The Dreaming Lady," "The House of Clocks," "The Doctor, His Wife and the Clock," "Missing Page 13," "Violet's Own."

_____ *Hand and Ring*. New York: G.P. Putnam's Sons, 1883.

_____ *Initials Only*. New York: Dodd, Mead and Company, 1911.

_____ *The Leavenworth Case*. New York: G.P. Putnam's Sons, 1878. Reprinted: Upper Saddle River, New jersey: Literature House, 1970.

_____ *Lost Man's Lane*. New York: G.P. Putnam's Sons, 1898.

_____ *A Matter of Millions*. New York: R. Bonner's Sons, 1891.

_____ *Mystery of the Hasty Arrow*. New York: Dodd, Mead and Company, 1917.

_____ *One of My Sons*. New York: G.P. Putnam's Sons, 1901.

_____ *The Step on the Stair*. New York: Dodd, Mead and Company, 1923.

_____ *A Strange Disappearance*. New York: G.P. Putnam's Sons, 1880.

_____ *That Affair Next Door*. New York: G.P. Putnam's Sons, 1897.

Messac, Regis. *Le Detective Novel*. Geneva: Slatkine, 1975. Reprint of the 1929 edition.

Chapter Six

Notes

[1]For churches where marriages are recorded see S.W. Phoenix, *The Whitney Family of Connecticut*. New York: Columbia University Press, 1878. II, 1518.

[2]Letter dated 5 August 1981 from the clerk of South Congregational Church, Margaret M. Crawford, lists Charles Rohlfs' baptism at that church on March 9, 1875; the marriage of AKG and Charles Rohlfs as November 25, 1884, and the baptism of their children, Rosamund and Sterling, on June 27, 1887. For records of the Rohlfs' participation in church affairs in Buffalo, see *The Records of the First Presbyterian Church, Buffalo, N.Y.* (pamphlet published as a centennial exhibit).

[3]Five undated letters from RHL to AFG are included in the collection of AFG: Letters.

Sources

Abbott, Lyman. *The New Puritanism*. New York: Books for Libraries Press, 1972 (reprint of the 1897 edition).

Davis, David Brion. *Homicide in American Fiction*. Ithaca: Cornell University Press, 1957.

Douglas, Ann. *The Feminization of American Culture*. New York: Avon, 1977.

Green, Anna Katharine. "Anna Katharine Green Tells How She Manufactures Her Plots," *Literary Digest*, 58, 13 July 1918: 48.

⎯⎯ *Dark Hollow*. New York: Dodd, Mead and Company, 1914.

⎯⎯ *Doctor Izard*. New York: G.P. Putnam's Sons, 1895.

⎯⎯ *The House in the Mist*. Indianapolis: The Bobbs Merrill Company, 1905.

⎯⎯ *Initials Only*. New York: Dodd, Mead and Company, 1914.

⎯⎯ Letters. Personal Collection of Mary Rohlfs.

⎯⎯ *The Mill Mystery*. New York: G.P. Putnam's Sons, 1886.

⎯⎯ *The Millionaire Baby*. Indianapolis, The Bobbs Merrill Company, 1905.

⎯⎯ "Why Human Beings Are Interested in Crime," *The American Magazine*, 87 (February 1919): 38-39, 82-86.

Leitch, Addison. *A Layman's Guide to Presbyterian Beliefs*. Grand Rapids, Iowa: Zondervan Publishing House, 1967.

Chapter Seven

Note

[1]Mary Alice Rohlfs recalls that her mother-in-law preferred Victorian style dresses and accessories. (Interview: New York: 4 June 1979).

Sources

Beard, Mary R. *Women as a Force in History*. New York: Octagon Books, 1976.

Calder, Jennie. *Women and Marriage in Victorian Fiction*. New York: Oxford University Press, 1976.

Cornillon, John. "A Case for Violet Strange," *Images of Women in Fiction*. Ed. Susan K. Cornillon. Bowling Green, Ohio: Popular Press, 1973.

Crumpacker, Laurie. "Four Novels of Harriet Beecher Stowe: A Study in Androgeny," *American Novelists Revisited*. Ed. Fritz Fleischmann. Boston: G.K. Hall, 1982, pp. 78-106.

Eaken, Paul John. *The New England Girl*. Athens, Georgia: University of Georgia Press, 1976.

Fetterley, Judith. *The Resisting Reader*. Bloomington: Indiana University Press, 1978.

Green, Anna Katharine. Letters. (Collection of Mary Alice Rohlfs).

⎯⎯ *A Matter of Millions*. New York: R. Bonner's Sons, 1891.

⎯⎯ *The Mayor's Wife*. Indianapolis: Bobbs-Merrill Company, 1907.

⎯⎯ *Miss Hurd: An Enigma*. New York: G.P. Putnam's Sons, 1894.

⎯⎯ *The Mystery of the Hasty Arrow*. New York: Dodd, Mead, and Company, 1917.

⎯⎯ *One of My Sons*. New York: G.P. Putnam's Sons, 1901.

_____ "The Gray Madam" and "The Hermit of____ Street" in *A Difficult Problem and Other Stories, New York:* F.P. Lupton Publishing Company, 1900. Reprinted: New York: Garrett Press, 1969.

_____ "The House of Clocks" In *The Golden Slipper* and *Other Problems for Violet Strange.* New York: Dodd, Mead and Company, 1912.

_____ "Shall He Wed Her?" in *The Old Stone House* and *Other Stories.* New York: G.P. Putnam's Sons, 1891. Reprinted: Freeport, New York: Books for Libraries Press, 1970.

_____ *That Affair Next Door.* New York: G.P. Putnam's, 1897,

Habeggar, Alfred. *Gender, Fantasy, and Realism in American Literature.* New York: Columbia University Press, 1982.

McCabe, John D. *Lights and Shadows of New York Life.* New York: Farrar, Straus, and Giroux, 1970.

Shaplen, Robert. *Free Love and Heavenly Sinners.* New York: Albert Knopf, 1954.

Ryan, Mary, *The Empire of Mother.* New York: Haworth Press, 1982.

Tuttleton, James. *The Novel of Manners in America.* Chapel Hill: University of North Carolina Press, 1972.

Warren, Joyce. *The American Narcissuss.* New Brunswick, New Jersey: Rutgers University Press, 1984.

Afterword
Source
Haycraft, Howard. *Murder for Pleasure.* New York: D. Appleton-Century Company, 1941.

Bibliography

Works of Anna Katharine Green

Novels:

The Leavenworth Case. New York: G.P. Putnam's Sons, 1878. Reprinted: Upper Saddle River, New Jersey: Literature House, 1970.

A Strange Disappearance. New York: G.P. Putnam's Sons, 1880.

XYZ. New York: G.P. Putnam's Sons, 1883.

Hand and Ring. New York: G.P. Putnam's Sons, 1883.

The Mill Mystery. New York: G.P. Putnam's Sons, 1886.

7 to 12. New York: G.P. Putnam's Sons, 1887.

Behind Close Doors. New York: G.P. Putnam's Sons, 1888.

The Forsaken Inn. New York: R. Bonner's Sons, 1890. Reprinted: Freeport, New York: Books for Libraries Press, 1971.

A Matter of Millions. New York: R. Bonner's Sons, 1891.

Cynthia Wakeham's Money. New York: G.P. Putnam's Sons, 1892.

Marked "Personal". New York: G.P. Putnam's Sons, 1893.

Miss Hurd—An Enigma. New York: G.P. Putnam's Sons, 1894.

Dr. Izard. New York: G.P. Putnam's Sons, 1895.

The Doctor, His Wife, and the Clock. New York: G.P. Putnam's Sons, 1895.

That Affair Next Door. New York: G.P. Putnam's Sons, 1897.

Lost Man's Lane. New York: G.P. Putnam's Sons, 1898.

Agatha Webb. New York: G.P. Putnam's Sons, 1899.

The Circular Study. New York: McClure, Phillips and Company, 1900. Reprinted: New York: Garland Publishing Company, 1976.

One of My Sons. New York: G.P. Putnam's Sons, 1901.

The Filigree Ball. Indianapolis: Bobbs-Merrill Company, 1903. Reprinted: New York: Arno Press, 1976.

The Millionaire Baby. Indianapolis: The Bobbs-Merrill Company, 1905.

The House in the Mist. Indianapolis: The Bobbs-Merrill Company, 1905.

The Amethyst Box. Indianapolis: The Bobbs-Merrill Company, 1905.

The Woman in the Alcove. Indianapolis: The Bobbs-Merrill Company, 1906.

The Chief Legatee. New York: Authors and Newspapers Association, 1907.

The Mayor's Wife. Indianapolis: The Bobbs-Merrill Company, 1907.
The Sword of Damocles. New York: G.P. Putnam's Sons, 1909.
Three Thousand Dollars. Boston: R.G. Badger, 1910.
The House of the Whispering Pines. New York: G.P. Putnam's Sons, 1910.
Initials Only. New York: Dodd, Mead and Company, 1911.
Dark Hollow. New York: Dodd, Mead and Company, 1914.
To the Minute, Scarlet and Black. New York: G.P. Putnam's Sons, 1916.
Mystery of the Hasty Arrow. New York: Dodd, Mead and Company, 1917.
The Step on the Stair. New York: Dodd, Mead and Company, 1923.

Short Story Collections
The Old Stone House and Other Stories. New York: G.P. Putnam's Sons, 1891.
    Reprinted: Freeport, New York: Books for Libraries Press, 1970. Contents:
    "The Old Stone House," "A Memorable Night," "The Black Cross,"
    "A Mysterious Case," "Shall He Wed Her."
A Difficult Problem and Other Stories. New York: F.P. Lupton Publishing
    Company, 1900. Reprinted: New York: Garrett Press, 1969. Contents:
    "A Difficult Problem," "The Gray Madam," "The Bronze Hand,"
    "Midnight in Beauchamp Row," "The Staircase at the Heart's Delight,"
    "The Hermit of—Street."
Masterpieces of Mystery. New York: Dodd, Mead and Company, 1912. Contents:
    "Midnight in Beauchamp Row," "Room No. 3," "The Ruby and The
    Caldron," "The Little Steel Coils," "The Staircase at the Heart's Delight,"
    "The Amethyst Box," "The Grey Lady," "The Thief," "The House in
    the Mist."
The Golden Slipper and Other Problems for Violet Strange. New York: G.P.
    Putnam's Sons, 1915. Contents: "The Golden Slipper," "The Second
    Bullet," "The Intangible Clew," "The Grotto Spectre," "The Dreaming
    Lady," "The House of Clocks," "The Doctor, His Wife and the Clock,"
    "Missing Page 13," "Violet's Own."

Drama:
Risifi's Daughter, A Drama. New York: G.P. Putnam's Sons, 1887.

Poetry
The Defense of the Bride and Other Poems. New York: G.P. Putnam's Sons,
    1882.

Selected Bibliography
Collins, Wilkie. "Wilkie Collins on the *Leavenworth Case*," *The Critic*, 22,
    28 January 1893, 52.

Green, Anna Katharine. "Anna Katharine Green Tells How She Manufactures her Plots," *Literary Digest*, 58 (13 July 1918): 48.

—— . "Why Human Beings Are Interested in Crime," *American Magazine*, 87 (1919): 38-39, 82-86.

Maio, Kathleen L. "Anna Katharine Green," *American Women Writers*. Ed. Linda Mainero. New York: Frederick Ungar Publishing Company, 1981. III: 498-500.

Mooney, Joan M. "Best Selling American Detective Fiction," *Armchair Detective*, 3 (1970): 98-103.

Murch, Alma E. *The Development of the Detective Novel*. Westport, Conn.: Greenwood Press, 1981.

"Noted Buffalonians, Wed Half Century Ago, Happy," *Courier-Express*, 18 November 1934, 1-2.

Phoenix, S.W. *The Whitney Family of Connecticut*. New York: Columbia University Press, 1878. I: 712-713; II: 1518.

Woodward, Kathleen. "Anna Katharine Green," *Bookman*, 70, October 1929, 168-170.

Index

Adams, Hilda, 52
The American Narcissus, 91
Astor, Mrs. John Jacob, 10
Auden, W. H., 16
Baldwin, Stanley, 27
Beard, Mary R., 101
Beecher, Henry Ward, 20, 79, 90
Besant, Walter, 27
Blackstone, Sir William, 101
Bok, Edward, 29
Braddon, Mary Elizabeth, 5
Brooklyn Eagle, The,
Brooklyn Heights, 19-20
Bucket, Inspector, 7
"The Buckled Bag," (Rinehart), 53
Bunyan, John, 87
Butterworth, Amelia, 1, 51, 52, 56, 62-69, 73, 92, 104
Buffalo, 21, 26, 50, 104
Byrd, Horace, 56, 60
Calder, Jennie, 93, 98, 101
Calvinism, 51, 82, 83, 88
Cawelti, John, 48
Cenci, The (Shelley), 37
Champigney, Robert, 54
Christie, Agatha, 12, 51
Circular Study, The (Rinehart), 52
Clark, Robert, 28
Collins, Wilkie, 2, 4, 7, 13, 23, 26
Cooper, James Fenimore, 5, 13
Cornillon, John, 90, 93
Coultrap-McQuin, 6
Crumpacker, Laurie, 89, 92
Cuff, Sergeant, 7
"Crossing Brooklyn Ferry" (Whitman), 18

Daly, Augustin, 25-26, 37-38
Daly, Joseph, 25
Davis, David B., 8, 79
Detective Fiction: appeal 10;
   confrontation drama, 16;
   conventions, 46, 48;
   detectives, 56;
   locked-room; motifs, 11;
   puzzle structure, 11; 48-49
Dicey, A. C., 27
Dickens, Charles, 7, 13
Dime Novel, 5
Douglas, Ann, 79
Doyle, Arthur Conan, 1, 14, 29
Dupin, Auguste, 6, 80
Dumas, Alexander, 5
Dwyer, Galbraith Welch, 29
East Haddam, 9, 98
East Lynne, 5
Eaken, Paul, 94
Edwards, Jonathan, 87
Emerson, Ralph Waldo, 31-32
The Empire of Mother, 90
Female Poets of America, 31-32
*The Feminization of
   American Culture, 79*
Fetterley, Judith, 13, 94
Fiedler, Leslie 13
The Fireside Companion, 5
First Presbyterian Church, 26, 79
The Four Hundred, 10
Freeman, Mary Wilkins, 29
Gilbert, Sandra and
   Susan Gilbert, 31-32
Gaboriau, Emile, 1, 6-7, 11, 23
Grace (state of), 78, 83
Green, Anna Katherine: agent, 29;
   children 26-27, 29, 30, 73;
   death, 104;
   education, 9, 21, 23;
   drama, 36-37;

gender roles, 89-103;
home in Buffalo, 39;
houses in fiction, 49-50;
marriage (Charles Rohlfs), 23-30;
mechanical devices in fiction,
    50-51;
name change from "Catherine", 22;
noveletes, 39-41;
parentage, 18;
poetry, 31-36;
prose style, 53-55;
religion, 78-79;
short fiction, 38-39; 41-45;
stepmother, 21;
siblings, 18, 22;
European trip, 27-28;
use of doubles, 52;
values, 80
Works:
Agatha Webb, 29, 69-71
The Amethyst Box, 30
Behind Closed Doors, 26, 48
"The Bronze Hand", 42, 50
The Chief Legatee, 30
The Circular Study, 30, 50,
    67-68
Cynthia Wakeham's Money, 28
Dark Hollow, 30, 52, 71-72
That Affair Next Door, 29-30
The Defense of the Bride, 23, 31-36
The Doctor, His Wife, and The Clock,
    28, 39, 40, 76
"The Dreaming Lady", 75
Dr. Izard, 28, 82-84
The Filigree Ball, 30, 50
The Forsaken Inn, 28, 39, 49
The Golden Slipper, 53, 73, 74-75
"The Gray Madam", 98
"The Grotto Spectre", 76-77
Hand and Ring, 23, 48, 62

The Hasty Arrow, 57;
"The Hermit of—Street", 94-95
"The House in the Mist", 30;
"The House of Clocks", 76, 96
"The House in the Mist", 49, 86-87,
    88
The House of the Whispering Pines,
    39, 52
Miss Hurd: An Enigma
The Leavenworth Case (novel):
    characters, 12-13, 51, 80, 90;
    first novel, 2, 4-17;
    popularity, 38;
    puzzle, 11-12;
    publication of, 1, 23;
    sales, 4;
    setting, 49;
The Leavenworth Case (drama), 37
Initials Only, 85-86
"The Little Steel Coils", 41, 50
Lost Man's Lane, 29, 48, 65-67
Marked Personal, 28
A Matter of Millions, 28, 49,
    60-61
The Mayor's Wife, 50, 99, 100-101
"Midnight in Beauchamp Row",
    42-43
The Mill Mystery, 26, 81, 94-96
The Millionaire Baby, 30, 81-82
Miss Hurd: An Enigma, 28, 101-103
"An Intangible Clue", 76
The Mystery of the Hasty Arrow,
    30, 72-73, 99
"The Old Stone House", 29, 39, 49
One of My Sons, 30, 46-47,
    70-71, 97
One Hour More, 39, 40
Risifi's Daughter, 36-37
"Room Number Three", 42
7 to 12, 26, 39
"The Second Bullet", 75-76

"Shall He Wed Her", 96-97
"Staircase at Heart's Delight",
    43-45, 61-62
A Step on the Stair, 30, 50, 98
A Strange Disappearance, 23,
    60-61, 90
The Sword of Damocles, 58
That Affair Next Door, 63-65, 99
Three Thousand Dollars, 39, 40
To The Minute, Scarlet and Black,
    30
"Violet's Own", 77
The Woman in the Alcove, 30,
    49, 71
XYZ, 23
Green, Annie, 22
Green, Katherine Ann Whitney, 18,
    20
Green, Frederick, 18
Green, Henry Ward Beecher Green,
    20
Green, James, 18, 22
Green, James Wilson 18-20; 24,
    25, 58
Green, Sarah Elizabeth, 19, 21, 22,
    26, 63, 95-96, 98
Green, Sidney, 19, 22, 96
Griswold, Rufus, 31-32
Gryce, Ebenezer, 57-73, 104:
    and Amelia Butterworth, 62-68;
    and Caleb Sweetwater, 59, 68-71;
    first case, 59-60;
    method, 14-16, 59;
    persona, 7, 58-59;
    and Poirot, 1, 51, 67;
    serial appearances, 56;
    and Sherlock Holmes, 1;
    source, 57-58;
Habeggar, Alfred, 93, 103
Halsey, Harlan P., 5
Hawthorne, Rose, 84

Hawthorne, Nathaniel, 1, 84,
    85, 87
Haycraft, Howard, 6, 104-105
Higginson, T.W., 33
Holmes, Sherlock, 1, 14, 80
Innis, Rachel, 1
Irving, Washington, 5, 42
Jackson, Helen Hunt, 33
Johnson, Rossiter, 22
The Ladies Companion, 5
The Ladies World, 5
Lady Audley's Secret (Braddon),
    5
L'Affaire Lerouge (Gaboriau),
    6
Larcom, Lucy, 33
Lecoq, M., 7
Lupin, Arsene, 80
Lyman, Reverend Albert, 23
Leavenworth, Eleanore, 11, 16
Leavenworth, Horatio, 11, 16
Leavenworth, Mary, 11, 16, 58, 80
Marple, Jane, 1, 51
McAllister, Ward, 10
McCabe, James D., 98, 99
Messac, Regis, 56
Mother of Detective Fiction, 1, 4,
    105
Mooney, Joan, 51
Murch, Alma E., 1, 4, 5-6,
Murder of Roger Ackroyd, The
    (Christie), 67
Murder on the Orient Express
    (Christie), 51
Mysterious Affair at Styles, The
    (Christie), 51
"My Kinsman, Major Molineau"
    (Hawthorne), 87
New York: environment, 1, 4-5,
    46-48;
    immigrants, 11;

police, 7 44
society, 5, 8, 10, 105;
Novels of Manners in America, 13
Old Sleuth, 5
Patriarchs, 10
Patton, George, 52, 54-55
Pere Tabaret, 6
Pilgrim's Progress (Bunyan), 87
Plymouth Church, 18, 20, 79, 90
Poe, Edgar Allan, 2, 6, 11, 41, 51
Poirot, Hercule, 1, 51, 67
The Poets and Poetry of America, 32
Presbyterian, 62, 78, 79
Providence, 78, 80, 84
Puritan, 78, 79, 82, 87, 88
"The Purloined letter" (Poe), 6, 16
Putnam, George, 4, 5, 22, 23
Raymond, Everett, 12-14, 16
Regeneration, 78
The Resisting Reader, 94
Ripley College,, 9, 21, 32
Rinehart, Mary Roberts, 30, 51, 52-58
Rohlfs, Charles, 23-30, 50, 79:
    actor, 23-24, 37;
    furniture designer, 27-28
Rohlfs, Fredericke Hunte, 23, 26
Rohlfs, Peter, 23;
Rohlfs, Roland, 27, 29

Rohlfs, Rosamund, 26, 30, 73
Rohlfs, Sterling, 26, 29, 30
Root, Elihu, 89
Ryan, Mary, 90
The Scarlet Letter, 84
Scott, Sir Walter, 5
Shelley, Percy, 37
Silver, Maud, 1-2,
South Congregational Church, 23, 24
Strange, Violet, 1, 53-55, 56, 92, 96, 104
Sweetwater, Caleb, 56, 68-71
Tabaret, Pere, 7
Ten Little Indians (Christie), 51
Tilton, Edward, 90
Tilton, Elizabeth, 90
Tuttleton, James, 13, 96
Vanderbilt, Mrs. Henry, 10
Walker, Cheryl, 32, 33-34
Warren, Joyce, 90, 92
Wells, Carolyn, 50, 51
Wentworth, Patricia, 1
Wharton, Edith Jones, 9, 13
Whitman, Walt, 18
Wood, Mrs. Henry, 5
Women: authors, 6, 51;
    roles of, 13, 89-103
Women as a Force in History, 101